THE OLD CHÂTEAU AND THE VILLAGE STREET

Two Vagabonds in Languedoc

"Here is an attempt to make a portrait, or rather a collective portrait, like one of those pictured by an old Flemish master. Here is a portrait of the French village of Janac in Upper Languedoc..."

Part painting in prose, part delightful narrative, this book is filled with clever observations, memorable characters and the authors' own paintings and drawings. It will prove irresistible to anyone interested in the culture of the French village.

THE KEGAN PAUL TRAVELLERS SERIES

A Journey Through Persia and Turkish Armenia • *Gerald Reitlinger*
A Summer in Touraine • *Frederic Lees*
George Sand & Frederick Chopin in Majorca • *George Sand*
A Woman in the Balkans • *Winifred Gordon*
Adventure in Hawaii and Tahiti • *Edward T. Perkins*
Alexandria: The Ancient and Modern Town • *E. Breccia*
Autobiography of a Chinese Girl • *Hsieh Ping-Ying*
Two Vagabonds in Languedoc • *Jan Gordon and Cora J. Gordon*
Burma • *R. Talbot Kelly*
Chinese Pictures • *J. F. Bishop*
Egypt and Nubia • *J. A. St. John*
Fifty Years in Maoriland • *James T. Pinfold*
In Hawaii with Jack London • *Jack London*
In Stevenson's Samoa • *Marie Fraser*
Island Nights' Entertainments • *Robert Louis Stevenson*
Man and Animals in the New Hebrides • *John R. Baker*
Mongolia • *N. Prejevalsky*
My Consulate in Samoa • *William B. Churchward*
News from Tartary • *Peter Fleming*
Oceania • *Frank Fox*
Unbeaten Tracks in Japan • *Isabella Lucy Bird*
Old Touraine • *Theodore Andrea Cook*
The Discovery of Tahiti • *George Robertson*
The French Riviera • *Pierre Devoluy and Pierre Borel*
The Golden Chersonese • *Isabella Lucy Bird*
The Heart of the Orient • *Michael Myers Shoemaker*
The Riviera • *Hugh Macmillan*
The Romance of Treasure Trove • *Charles R. Beard*
To Lhasa in Disguise • *William Montgomery McGovern*
Treasure of Ophir • *C. E. V. Craufurd*
A Year Amongst the Persians • *Edward Granville Browne*
Constantinople and Istanbul Old and New • *H. G. Dwight*
Tahiti • *George Calderon*
Cruise of the Snark • *Jack London*
In the South Seas • *Robert Louis Stevenson*
Six Months in Hawaii • *Isabella Bird*
Korea and Her Neighbours • *Isabella Bird*
Strolling Through Istanbul • *H. Sumner-Boyd and J. Freely*
Camp Life and Sport in Dalmatia and the Herzegovina • *Anonymous*
Quest for Sheba • *Norman Stone Pearn and Vernon Barlow*
An English Consul in Siam • *W. A. R. Wood*
South Sea Idyls • *Charles Warren Stoddard*
Hawaii: The Past, Present and Future of its Island-Kingdom • *Gerald Manly Hopkins*

Two Vagabonds in Languedoc

BY
JAN & CORA J. GORDON

LONDON AND NEW YORK

First published in 2005 by
Kegan Paul Limited

Published 2013 by Routledge
2 Park Square, Milton Park, Abingdon, Oxfordshire OX14 4RN
711 Third Avenue, New York, NY 10017, USA

First issued in paperback 2016

Routledge is an imprint of the Taylor & Francis Group, an informa business

© Kegan Paul, 2005

All Rights reserved. No part of this book may be reprinted or reproduced or utilised in any form or by any electric, mechanical or other means, now known or hereafter invented, including photocopying or recording, or in any information storage or retrieval system, without permission in writing from the publishers.

British Library Cataloguing in Publication Data

Library of Congress Cataloging-in-Publication Data
Applied for.

ISBN 13: 978-1-138-98632-9 (pbk)
ISBN 13: 978-0-7103-1008-8 (hbk)

TO
HERMINE AND FRITZ VANDERPYL
IN RECOGNITION OF OUR LONG-
STANDING FRIENDSHIP

CONTENTS

CHAPTER		PAGE
I.	Our Last Breakfast in Upper Languedoc	1
II.	Recollections on a Green Garden Seat	21
III.	Mine Host and Hostess of the Hôtel Sestrol	40
IV.	The *Juge de Paix* and the Court of Janac	67
V.	Peasants and Villagers—Life and Customs	91
VI.	Eaters and Eaten, and Gastronomic Things	116
VII.	The Strange Case of Monsieur Lemoule	139
VIII.	The Mountain Fires around the Village	152
IX.	Four Days of Village Festival	171
X.	The Ancient Church and its Latter-day Patrons	191
XI.	Magic and Medicine—Health and Hygiene	209
XII.	. . . And the Fruits in their Seasons	225
XIII.	Adieu . . . Adieu !	239

LIST OF ILLUSTRATIONS

PLATES BY CORA GORDON

	FACING PAGE
THE OLD CHÂTEAU AND THE VILLAGE STREET	*Frontispiece*
JANAC FROM OUR BACK GARDEN	8
THE LONG STREET OF JANAC	14
JANAC FROM THE OLD FORTRESS	22
MAIN STREET OF JANAC	28
THE ROAD WHICH CONTOURS JANAC MILL	38
JANAC FROM THE HILLSIDE	164
PLACE DU GRIFOULES	176
THE RIVER VALLEY FROM THE DOCTOR'S GARDEN	214

ILLUSTRATIONS IN THE TEXT

	PAGE
THE ROAD INTO JANAC	11
GANGS OF SPANIARDS	24
THE BROKEN LEG	32
SESTROL'S SNOWING UP	44
THE SCARE	47
IN THE RIVER-BED	49
HAT BOOTH IN A COUNTRY FAIR	53
BLOCKED UP THE SPIGOTS OF THE FOUNTAIN	63
THE ANGER OF MONSIEUR TREE-FROG	70
THE MURDERESS	78
THE VILLAGE COURT	83
TOASTING EACH OTHER IN PINARD	87

LIST OF ILLUSTRATIONS

	PAGE
VEGETABLES	96
THE UMBRELLA MENDERS	112
THE FLAILERS	118
THE OX DOCK	121
TUK-TUK	127
CUPBOARD LOVE ON BOTH SIDES	136
THE FIRE IN THE BRUSH	159
THEORETICAL PAINTING!	161
THE OLD PIGEON LOFT	166
THE FIRE-ENGINE	169
THE PROCESSION	179
MONSIEUR DIADÈME'S PLAN	182
LA TOGNE	186
PLAYING FOR FUNDS	189
NEAR MARTINOLLES	193
THE SCHOOLMASTER'S WIFE AND GOAT	194
THE CHURCH OF JANAC	197
BLESSING THE ANIMALS	204
THE OLD MILL OF JANAC	213
THE SULPHATER	231

TWO VAGABONDS IN LANGUEDOC

TWO VAGABONDS IN LANGUEDOC

I

OUR LAST BREAKFAST IN UPPER LANGUEDOC

HERE is an attempt to make a portrait, or rather a collective portrait, like one of those pictured corporations by an old Flemish master. Here is a portrait of the French village of Janac in Upper Languedoc, taken from the door of the Hôtel Sestrol. You will perceive in the centre the figures of Monsieur and Madame Sestrol and their son Raymond; grouped about them are the baker, the blacksmith, the shoemaker, the *épicier*-cobbler, the ex-American soldier, the mad priest, the *garde champêtre*, the *juge de paix*, etc., fading into a mass of villagers and peasantry, some suggested, others merely indicated. The picture, admittedly, suffers from the disadvantages of the portrait—it is seen from one angle only and in one lighting.

Our friend Boanerges, well-known art critic and gastronomer of Paris, has the queer hobby of collecting himself in facsimile from the hands of all his painter friends. These portraits he hangs regimented in his study, a dozen presentments overlook the original at his work: a dozen Boanerges frown; smile; look indifferent, self-satisfied, absorbed or reflective upon the Boanerges who is grumbling over his manuscript. Of these many portraits all resemble the original, yet none are like each other: they are as the many facets of a jewel, each has its own peculiar glint, none have the same glint, yet all are of the same jewel.

We submit this book to such limitations of portrait work. It is seen at an angle, it has only one lighting, it gives, we hope, at least one glint of the jewel, and it includes little which was behind us or out of sight. Humble jog-trotters we have attempted no "simultanism." Yet we feel that, admitted the defects of portraiture, a truth may be obtained by one steady look from one chosen angle in some ways as truthful as may be a more comprehensive presentation such as a fully moulded bust.

If this book can but bring the reader a little into an easier contact with the fascinating genius of the French village we shall be content.

A modern poetess, of Hampstead we believe, opened her plaintive lament with the line: "I have no physical need of a chair." So might we borrow or transpose her verse into: We have no physical need of an alarum-clock.

We can despise that assemblage of wheels and springs which may keep you awake with its monotonous beating of the passage of time—the tom-tom of eternity—but which, come morning, may forget to awaken you, if you yourself have forgotten to wind the hammer spring. *We* have no need of such an implement. Our alarum-clock is spontaneous and natural; it works without forethought on our part, indeed, the less the forethought the more sure the action. Nor has our alarum-clock the drawbacks of a mechanical one. It does not arouse us with abrupt and horrid jangle, startling us from some sweet unconcluded dream, introducing the day with cacophony. No. Our clock merges sleep into wakefulness, gradating our dream for us as slumber steals from the mind. Nor can our clock be shut off with the aggravated hand of a snoozer impatient to resume the futile attempt of restringing dream jewels which the broken thread of sleep has scattered. Our awakener operates gently but remorselessly, first drawing away slumber as the veils are taken from a Moslem bride; then, however, rousing us moment by moment into true wakefulness, nay, into sheer muscular activity, the only solution of which is to get up. Not only is sleep banished but the wakefulness is firmly enthroned in the mind's high places and so no remedy is there for it; up we must get.

As a *mere* awakener the sun has some merits. Phœbus Apollo peering over the crest of the hill and tapping you upon the nape of the neck with a long warm finger, reminding you that a new day has come, is perhaps the most pleasant of " knockers up." But Phœbus is a poor hand at getting you from bed. He is about as effective as the sleepy elbow of a warm and drowsy wife. He will awaken you, but only to enjoy the cosy delight of that twilight of the mind where reverie dances with dream in a golden haze. No, the sun is not effective as a " knocker up," however pleasant it may be.

The sun is the only awakener we do not detest, and we do not detest him because he does not insist upon our getting up. We don't mind being awakened; but the stirring into activity annoys us. So all effective arousers must earn dislike. I confess that we heartily loathe our alarum-clock, no matter how tactful he may be. But greater than we loathe him the Government loathes him. His portrait is writ up large, magnified fifty times upon the walls of the Mairie, all good citizens are conjured to exterminate him at sight, he does dreadful things to one's children and is peculiarly vicious towards babies. But, bless you, notices of that sort don't mean anything here. The peasant takes no notice. The babies die and the flies flourish at their will. No dung or refuse is protected from them, and one might as well offer the peasant a whole Utopia at once as to suggest that the number of flies could be diminished with a little forethought. The only remedy used against them is that of closing both windows and shutters so that through the livelong day the interior of the house stews in an airless gloom during the heat of the summer, while the flies, hating darkness like all sensible creatures, dance the saraband, wax fat and multiply in the sun.

The flies having awoken me I lie contemplating, with a dreamy eye, our room. The flies have not yet badgered me to an exasperated leap from bed; I dodge them for a while by turning my face to the shadow. They wander over my hair in a distracted, puzzled manner, not yet realizing that that most delectable of playgrounds, the nose, has been turned away from the light. What *is* the use of a million eyes, I wonder?

My point of perspective is low, since my couch is on the floor. To one side of me towers the wooden front of the bed proper which, though heavily built and apparently cumbersome, proved too narrow for easy double sleeping and so ejected me to my hard and lowly position. Jo sleeps in state on the boxspring mattress. I have the down mattress, on the boards, and we have divided the bedclothes, supplementing them when necessary with overcoats, sweater, jumpers, etc. From where I lie I have long noted a peculiarity in this massive bed head. The post upon one side is carved and moulded, upon the other side it is angular and plain. This marks a habit in the country, that of setting the bed in an alcove shrouded with curtains to avoid all chance of the dreaded *courant d'air*, and so as only one side of the bed should be visible only one side needs decoration, thus combining beauty with economy; but our poor bed, plucked from its alcove and set rudely thus in an open room, looks something as uncomfortable as a hermit crab without a shell. I have seen on the cinematograph one such sea creature dance with joy at housing its edible tail in a suitable receptacle, so one might imagine our bed capering clumsily with delight at hiding its undecorative edge in an appropriate recess.

Our room is some eleven or twelve feet square and perhaps nine feet high, so we are not cramped. It is gay because it has two windows which look out on to a valley, deep cut and covered on the far side with chestnut trees, some green, others already yellowing with autumn, while yet others, standing together in a group, are the colour of old and faded gilding, dead, burned at their posts like the soldiers of Pompeii. Our room is of sober colour, because the wallpaper is that mixture of umber grey and dingy green which the French call *pratique*: that is to say, it can absorb years of dirt without an appreciable change of colour.

Our room is furnished: a round table covered with a cloth (*pratique* colour too), a couple of chairs, a large trunk (locked), a brown cupboard (full), a washstand and a *table de nuit* (empty) complete, with the bed, our hired furniture, to which we have added a deck-chair bought in Toulouse from a furniture dealer who on his business cards also proclaimed himself " *licencié en droit*," a fledgling lawyer who evidently had found it more profitable to furnish unions than to furbish disunions. The locked trunk and the full cupboard are reminiscences of our predecessor. He was, we learned, a " contrairy " man with a white beard which was a full yard long, and he has continued his contrairiety after his death by cumbering our apartment with his effects which our hosts, the Sestrols, must guard till the relatives have made up their minds whether the succession to them is worth the trouble of accepting or no. So both the cupboard in our room and the cupboard in the room outside are cumbered with his things, clothes offering bait to the moth, sportsman's truck long gone rusty, a gramophone with a worn-out spring, and so on.

Our own effects stand about, half piled, half packed, for this is our last day in Janac.

This evening we shall bid *adieu* to Janac, probably for ever. We have spent four months in this little lost village of Northern Languedoc; four quiet full months. We came for a few weeks at the outside, but have lingered on, always finding new things of interest, always finding more subjects to paint; to the great astonishment of the villagers themselves, who cannot understand what retains us when we are free to go elsewhither. Our summer has come to an end. Not boredom, but the chills of high October, and perhaps the dread of new wine and of "*stoffee,*" are urging us back to Paris, back to Montparnasse and to the warmth of our studio stove.

The flies are now raiding us persistently for breakfast. Their dreadful note " Brr-zz-p " sounds the introduction to an exasperating tickle; and so we slap ourselves into a daytime mood when it is no longer luxury but sloth to lie between sheets. Jo is not one of your women who consider dressing a sacrament. She does not wholly consider that the first duty of womankind is to give pleasure only in the exteriors, nor is she one who will spend at least four hours a day to decorate her body when she will not spend ten minutes to decorate her mind; making of her person a canvas, herself a picture (often badly composed) and of the whole world a mere exhibition room. A quarter of an hour and we are ready to front our last day in Janac, hungry for our final breakfast.

Our house is set bodily into the side of the hill. Below us is a stable, half blasted from the rock. As we went to bed last night, the little black horse stamped his feet beneath us. When we first came here we were awakened by the shrill cries of a flock of little ducklings which would greet Madame Sestrol each morning with exclamations of hunger, to which our good hostess answered, "*Ritou, ritou,*" such being the proper form of addressing the little duck in Janac. Above us is a loft, its dark corners filled with the crumbling trash which humanity allows to accumulate, and to this loft I mount by a ladder while Jo descends to the road by the staircase. She is going to order breakfast while I am bound for the garden where I search the pergola for a last morning meal of grapes.

Our house is three stories high and the garden door is set a step or two up from the loft, so that in some sixteen or eighteen feet—which is the depth of the house—the hill has mounted two full stories and a piece, thus giving the normal slope of the ridge of Janac. The garden is burrowed out of the slope. Monsieur Sestrol has put the grape pergola at our disposition: "Eat as many as you see fit," he says; adding, "For my part, grapes don't interest me," while Raymond, the son, adds further: "Half a glass of wine is worth all the grapes in the world." So every morning, from that joyful one when we found the first ripened bunch, we have sauced our *café au lait* and dry bread with white grapes. The pergola has three stems. One gives us the sweet white grapes on which we have battened; one grows a large brownish grape which this year, for some reason, has gone mouldy and burst; one produces a small, intensely dark fruit with a juice which stains like blackberries, a grape which Monsieur Sestrol says " tastes like bugs, but makes good wine."

***

Ha! the sweet morning air. The cicada, new warmed by the rising sun, has just turned up his persistent ratchet, which, whirring unceasingly, makes the heat of the day seem much more hot and exhausting than the thermometer would imply.

From where I stand, reaching up to the grape vines, Janac appears merely a short perspective of shelving and dried gardens, a clump of nondescript roofs shrouded in acacia trees, over which towers on its conical hill the old fortress, first planted, they say, by the Gauls, but undistinguished till the latter part of the twelfth century, when it fell into the hands of Richard Comte de Poitiers, son of our Henry II, and became a meeting-place for the Count and the King of Aragon. Janac Castle looks a romantic place. The tall keep with its monstrous long arrow slits should be a mute witness of many a terrible siege, one hunts to find old records such as those which tell of the capture of other fortresses of which Fayban for instance, writes:

" The whiche persones beynge hedes of ye cytie conueyed theyr purpose in suche wyse y^{et} they turnyed y^e comons of y^{e}cytie upon the Englysshemen and sodaynly arose agayne theym and slew of theym many, and many toke prysoners. And as y^e Englysshemen fledde or faught by the streetes

JANAC FROM OUR BACK GARDEN

the womē and other feeble persons cast upon theme stones and hote lycours to theyr great confucion, so that the Englysshemen were in passynge myserie and desolacion."

Or again for an evacuation:

"And soon after the cytie of Bayons was geuen up by appointment, so that the solildyours shuld leve theyr armour behynd them. And for every woman there beynge was graunted a horse to ryde upon and to every horseman X scutis to pay for theyr costs; and to every foteman V without more by them to be taken."

It seems as if they had better fighting manners then than now.

But Janac records are silent of doughty deeds. Fifteen miles to the south-east the Castle of Thuries, considered impregnable, was captured by the Bastard de Mauleon with six comrades, as Froissart relates; twenty miles to the south-west Penne Castle was besieged by Simon de Montfort who as an old Provencal historian writes:

"Et quant no son estats arribats devant ladita Pena, le séty y an boutat, la ont fait adressar peyreras, calabres et autres engines per tirar contra ladita plassa; car forta era et imprenabla."

Penne held out till thirst reduced it. But Janac, alas, proud Castle, was handed about, boasting but one petty revolution against its overlord of Toulouse, a revolution which collapsed without any attempt at defence. Janac boasts no heroic history. It stands a monument without a memory. The larger part of it was bought in 1246 by Raymond of Toulouse for 20,000 sous of Cahors.

I clamber up the steep stone steps, open the gate made of old barrel staves and thus gain the path down which I come to the hangar which shelters the weekly market, to the blacksmith's shop and café, and to the house of the shoemaker, St. Mouxa, linear descendant of the old Seigneurs of Janac. It is strange how aristocratic a craft is shoemaking. At first sight not a very palatable profession, neither beeswax nor blacking seems the most acceptable of materials in which to work. Yet amongst the village craftsmen the shoemaker is something of a natural aristocrat; almost always he is the village free thinker, and free thought indicates a certain aristocratic attitude, since amongst men aristocracy and independence of control are synonymous. Lamb admits no halting point of dignified degeneration between king and beggar; true, one cannot imagine with comfort a king become waiter nor yet barber, but why not shoemaker? After all, shoemaking is not a servile trade, not village shoemaking at all events. He does not truckle to his customers, who must find feet to fit his boots or go limping and grow corns. At any rate, here you have an example, one of the old Aristocrats of France who were almost kings in their own country.

Another shoemaker lives in the upper village, an oldish man hirsute with that kind of beard which scatters in the wind; a man who, under a heavy slouched hat, has one joy in life, that of following every village corpse to the cemetery; no funeral in Janac is complete without him. I have merely brought him in here to supplement my reflections on the independence of cobbling thought. Janac had a band—a *fanfare* they call it, and from the detached specimens we have heard I bet the name was appropriate enough—the chemist was conductor, the old cobbler played some instrument of portentous brass. Janac has erected a monument to its dead heroes of the war, the *fanfare* made the festival noise to celebrate the unveiling, but the ceremony was concluded with a church service. Here the cobbler protested; as much celebration as you like but no church, he split the band on the question and so the *fanfare* is silent, wrecked on the dire subject of religion—which has before now laid dreadful hands on this district during the times of the Albigeois. The big drum, bought by subscription, lies

THE ROAD INTO JANAC.

unbeaten in the Mairie, locked in with the fire-engine by Raymond Sestrol, who is the Mayor's secretary.

Beyond the Seigneur-cobbler is a small yard closed by a grille, where was enacted the tragedy of Faust and the duckling—of which more later. The house backing the yard has no door on this side and the yard is only used as a slop-pail by the old woman who lives on the second story and who empties her buckets over the balcony railing; above her in an attic lives the mad priest. Next comes the bottling establishment of the blacksmith's brother, who has the homely sobriquet of "Potato"; and lastly is the home of Tuk-Tuk.

* *

Jo has done her duty; she is sitting at the table beneath acacia trees which overshadow the cement pavement before the Hôtel Sestrol. I pass her, enter the small dining-room of the Hôtel Sestrol, and through it come into the dimly lit kitchen where plump Marie Sestrol watches the milk with those lines of anxiety which any event, from this simple one to an unexpected absence of her husband, rules across her brows. She is grey haired and her face has almost an Indian tint, one feels that if her body had been left to Nature she would look like the head of one of the fatter Roman Emperors on a museum pedestal, but the would-be perfect pillar of her body had been deformed by that pitiless moulder, the country corset, strange implement of a bygone inquisition when the woman whose waist could not almost pass through the eye of a needle could by no means enter the kingdom of beauty. I greet Madame Sestrol and say:

"How is the leg this morning?"

"Ah," she replies, smiling, "it's not in the morning that it is painful, Monsieur Jean."

"Still," I answer, "you should be reposing, you know."

"Reposing indeed," answers Madame Sestrol, "and how would things get along without me, I'd like to know?" She grunts with disgust.

How many persons have not the peculiar satisfaction of believing themselves to be indispensable? Our good hostess has varicose veins. The doctor has told her to lie up for a few days. But no. The place could not get along without her. The same thing has happened to her before, earlier during the summer. She knows what will happen. But do humans learn by experience ? She will, as she did last time, prolong her resistance to the unavoidable till she has prolonged two or three days' voluntary rest into two or three weeks' compulsory absence. In order that her hotel shall not have to survive three days without its mistress it will have to survive a fortnight. This is true peasant philosophy towards illness. It is a reminiscence of that time when the village had no doctors, knew no medicine. Then was the true survival of the fittest. The peasant worked till he was carried to bed. It was "shame" to give way to an illness as it was "shame" to turn one's back upon an enemy and for the same reason, retreat in either case meant death or a vivid risk of death. To-day we ju-jitsu disease, but this method would seem as absurd to a peasant as would the Japanese theory of self-defence— to win by ceding.

Now and again when she was cutting up nettles for the ducklings, Madame Sestrol would condescend to raise her leg upon a chair, but she complained that the position was absurd and inconvenient. After a few minutes down came the leg again.

The kitchen in which she now stands is lit by a tiny window and two doors. It is small, yet contains two large iron stoves. There is not a spare space of wall unoccupied with utensils. Across one end hang huge cauldrons of copper, some beaten with intricate patterns of hammerwork, the largest fully three feet across, and all are polished till a hundred glints as of fire lighten the dark kitchen corners ; on the shelves stand grey pots of stoneware filled with the first article of culinary faith : as they say in church, " I believe in God the Father Almighty," so in this part of France they say in the kitchen, " I believe in goose grease."

The Hôtel Sestrol stands just opposite the house of Tuk-Tuk and therefore on the opposite side to all the houses which I passed on my way to breakfast, to the blacksmith's, to his café, to the Seigneur-shoemaker, to the mad priest, to Potato's and to Tuk-Tuk's. Here we reach the corner of a small triangular place, the hotel being at the lowest corner. The hotel itself stands with its back to the hill, so that to the road it presents two stories of prosperity shaded with acacia trees, while to the valley-side it uprears no less than four stories without a window. It is a narrow house and from the far hill looks not unlike a Roman brick set on edge.

So here we are sitting before our *café au lait* with our slab of dry bread for nourishment and our grapes for luxury.

The road is a favourite thoroughfare. Along it one travels to the chestnut woods; to the road which curls down the hill to the station; to the free school; to the bullock dock; to the vineyards and the hayfields. As we breakfast the peasants pass to and fro on their daily business. As they go they greet us with a cheerful Janac salute:

" Bon jour, m'sieur et dame, ça va l'appétit."

Then seeing us with our pile of luscious grapes before us they stop and pointing an accusing finger they say with French frankness :

" Ça purge, hein."

In this country of vineyards they cannot partake of the romantic feelings of the poor northerner eating grapes culled with his own hands. They look upon us with the eyes that we might fix upon a foreigner quaffing Eno's under the impression that he had discovered a delicious English summer refreshment. The prophet has no honour in his own country, so to be a true table delicacy the edible must be far from the vicinity of too easy production ; nature

THE LONG STREET OF JANAC

is not delectable unless she is somewhat rare, so the grape and the peach have no flavour better than in England, while in these countries of the South they might be surprised by a good English apple or pear.

To us bred up in the Victorian decencies there is a charm in the French frank acceptance of physical things. One's mind rejoices in the fact that there are no *sotto voce* subjects, that the processes of birth, death and life here are normal incidents and not improper mysteries. Yet one may confess also that the sudden qualification of the sensuous delight of the grape by a statement of its supposed medical functions does not at *this* moment increase our pleasure. We have no desire to follow the fruit further than the limits of flavour. We might say it does indeed not seem good taste to introduce the physiological at this moment. There is a time for reticence, in spite of all the acknowledged virtues of frankness. This is selection, not hypocrisy ; and, if gastronomy is an art, such selection should here be exercised.

The thrum of a motor-car is heard. Poking its nose uphill, labouring over the cobbles on the third speed the doctor's Citroën shows its bonnet round the corner. Immediately Jo's face assumes an expression of pained intensity. Half rising in her seat she cries out sharply, urgently :

"Come here, come here, sir ! Kissme ! Kissme ! Confound you ! "

A treble barking, a strident note which rips through the ear drum, answers her as a small khaki-coloured dog with bared teeth leaps from beneath our table to challenge the grey mechanical monster snorting across the triangle. The doctor clanks in the second speed, waves us a "*bon jour*," and is gone, while Kissme sneaks back to Jo's feet wagging the whole of its body from back of the forelegs to express a conviction that another grave danger has been kept off by vigilance and pluck. It is lucky, however, that the doctor does not know English.

We have now been four months in Janac, for four months we have thus breakfasted beneath the acacia trees at the door of the Hôtel Sestrol; but, till we have been able to pluck our grapes for ourselves, the Sestrols have always refused to give us fruit for breakfast. Or rather, they haven't exactly refused, but they have shown a peasant obtuseness in the matter. Fruit for lunch, when it is but silver, or fruit for supper, when it is lead—as the proverb says—they offer us in plenty. But golden morning fruit, healthy morning fruit, fruit which " purifies the blood " as *we* say. At any rate, even if we put aside fruit from supper, saying that would be excellent in the morning, when the morning comes it has disappeared. For a long while we have wondered whence came this reluctance to freshen our morning breakfast with strawberries or plums, with peaches or melon, as each came into season. At last we found that the peasant believes that fruit and milk are disturbing companions. We had milk in our coffee, therefore a demand for simultaneous fruit could only be the ignorance of a barbarian from that land which is so foggy that fruit never ripens. Here they know that fruit never ripens in England because London must stretch out long tentacles even as distantly as Janac, buying from afar the produce of her plum orchards and of her chestnut groves. We were being protected from ourselves.

* *
*

The morning sun shines full into the triangular place. It beats upon the shops of the baker and of the *épicier*-cobbler, strikes slantways across the front of Tuk-Tuk's, silvers the mica-schist roofing of the old barn and paints deep shadows under the eaves. We in shadow look out into a harmony of grey silver and of pale gold, variegated by the gay colours of the advertisements for Chocolat Menier, Crème Éclipse, Pâté lion Noir and so on which the *épicier* has nailed to his shutters and which flaunt a festival of colours as though the products of the factory were an occasion for rejoicing in the monotonous tints of the village existence. Before the sunk door of the barn a bullock cart is stationed and the owner of the barn is pitching manure into the cart. Below the waggon the chickens pick up scattered nastiness which is thus transmuted into delicacy for the towns. From Potato's establishment comes a continuous clatter as his assistant, Roman nosed like a Bourbon, spins the mechanical brush which cleans the empty beer bottles. The mad priest, shouldering a hoe and a sack, passes downhill, going to his little property which lies beyond the cemetery. His rusty hat looks as though it was made of the skins of kittens long drowned, his cape is as ragged as the edge of a rain-cloud, his *soutane* is patched with sewings of string and is soiled with the earth. Almost every time that he has passed us during four months we have found some peasant ready to explain: " Voilà—Il est fou ce prêtre-là."

The mother-in-law of the *garde champêtre* crosses the priest. She is another crazy character of the village. She has a flat face with china blue eyes which stare straight before her. She is tall, rigid and rusty, and when she walks she goes as if she were too rigid to balance herself. She reels a reckless course through the village, tottering about, and we have a continual terror that she will dive into our lap, or go head first over the parapet. Once she did pitch into the *lavoir*, but otherwise has avoided by some miracle a more serious accident. The villagers say that the priest went mad through sanctity, the woman through greed. Of

c

all her greeds, however, only one remains, that for coffee. She will do anything to gain a few sous, even petty larceny. This money she spends on coffee with which she hurries to some secluded country spot where in the shelter of a hedge she makes a small fire, brews her beverage and drinks it even to the last of the grounds. As she likes her coffee to be both dark coloured and copious her coffee-pot for preference is any old blacking tin.

It seems hard that our village should introduce itself first by its less responsible element, that the two chief bugbears of man, fanaticism and greed, should thus poke their heads over the barrier at us during the first hour of our last day. We have so many other varieties of men we might have called up, or a less differentiated series of women. Indeed, all the while we have been breakfasting a continual stream of the female sex has been moving down and up hill along the road across the far base of the triangular place. These women and girls walk each within a barrel hoop, an ingenious device for splaying out the buckets which they carry and thus prevent the water from splashing the skirt. For the most part these buckets which are carried thus, downhill to and uphill from the old fountain, are of beaten copper rather queer in shape like the crown of a battered top hat.

But talking about varieties of men in comparison with these women brings out a fact which I had not before noted, which is that while almost every man who passes has his particular character, each an individual although one may see him but once, these women and girls are emphatically a herd from which one only picks out the individuals by personal encounter. I have no doubt that individual for individual the women have as much inherent character as the men, but externally, superficially, it does not appear. Lest this should be thought mere masculine prejudice I have checked my observation by that of Jo : she, too, has noted this characteristic. Didn't somebody write a book entitled *Regiment of Women?* There you have it. These women are regimented, have no more individuality than a line of soldiers in spite of their diversity of dress. Some sergeant-major has had the handling of them, and we won't get to the back of the woman problem until we have hunted up and ousted the sergeant-major. As it is, when a man marries a normal woman he marries " on to the strength " as surely as does any woman who marries into barracks.

But, alas, this differentiation between women and men is becoming minimized, not indeed in this village—which to all intents and purposes has held its character since Gothic times—but in the towns, in the shadow of our new civilization of which the factory chimney is the Cleopatra's Needle. We are not ousting the sergeant-major from behind the regiment of women, but appointing a new officer behind a regiment of men. We are not making women more individual, but making men *mere* sheep. Meredith says " Women will be the last thing civilized by man." He would more truly have said " Man will be the last thing civilized by women." For to-day civilization means submission to the mass, loss of individuality, submergence in the herd, and so as the old proverb says " Extremes meet," the savage fast bound in the laws of " Taboo " can link hands with the modern man bound in the observances of " civilization." The woman has lost individual character because she has always been a factory worker, the home is a factory in miniature, a factory of men; her task is monotonous, reiterative and uninteresting. Like the factory worker she works without becoming aware of her production. Turning out a hundred pieces of metal to a fixed shape, in order to turn out a hundred similar pieces to-morrow, is like washing a family's dishes or mending its shirts in order to wash and mend again in the near future. The village workman is not tied thus to task. Instance the cooper. He keeps the tobacco shop, he has a series of scattered fields, some under grass, some planted with vines, some orcharded in plums, he has woods of chestnut, of brush. He is, in turn, farmer, vintner, tobacconist, woodcutter, carter, cooper. He is as changeable as the seasons, and when all other trades stand still one will find him lounging by the banks of the Aveyron, the *true* definition of an angler, a worm at one end and a very acute man at the other, while sleek Oursa—his black dog—steals behind him silent as if she were but a shadow which the real dog has mislaid.

II

RECOLLECTIONS ON A GREEN GARDEN SEAT

THIS morning we have no work to do. You cannot paint on the very day you are going away, because both the spirit is disturbed and the means of transporting a sticky canvas are cumbersome. Therefore we transfer ourselves from the breakfast table to a green garden seat which backs the wall of the Hôtel Sestrol. Here we sit lazily reviewing our past four months in Janac, breathing the air yet fresh with the chill of the night.

We discovered Janac as we discover almost all good things, by accident. Happily, nobody had told us to come to Janac. To a young painter lacking in the experience of "sketching corners," we can give a word of advice. Be wary of going to a place recommended by another painter. Not art but beauty is " nature seen through a temperament " ; each temperament does not perceive beauty in the same environment. Art is a double temperamental fusion : it is nature first seen through the temperament of appreciation, then re-created by the temperament of the craftsman. An " Artists' colony " is a contradiction in terms, being actually " one artist and a colony of sheep." The advice which led us to this forgotten corner of France was no broader than the mere designation of a locality. Our informant knew of our habit of wandering afoot, she merely indicated to us a starting-point for explorations—a point almost exactly bisecting a straight line between Marseilles and Bordeaux.

We went to her starting-point; we made a tour of fifteen days afoot over the hills and through the valleys of Upper Languedoc, we decided upon our future rests for the summer: one month in this place, six weeks in that, a fortnight farther on, and so forth. When the tour was over, our plans settled, our luggage packed for our first move . . . we happened on Janac one fine spring day. We came, we stayed. That is the history of our whole summer.

It was the map which brought us here. Hapless the man who does not know the delight of poring over a map. We had made a fifteen days' detour, describing, with our legs for compasses, a large irregular circle through the departments of Aveyron, Lot, Tarn et Garonne and Tarn, a fifteen days' ambulation over the circumference when the ideal spot which we were seeking was the centre itself. Having returned to our starting-point—where we had deposited our heavier baggage—we could not, of course, resist wandering again on the paper over the varied routes of our quest. Then it struck me that this place Janac, settled at the very centre of our circle, seemed *on the map* a very difficult place to reach. No road approached it in a frank and straight manner, they all came with the hesitancy and digressions of the proverbial cat. Only the railway made any attempt at cutting corners, and did so by plunging in and out of tunnels. The roads looked as if they had been set out by an embroiderer rather than by an engineer. So we decided to pay this elusive Janac a flying visit . . . to be sure of missing nothing.

We ourselves came to Janac by the railway. But we did not step out at Janac station. We looked out of the carriage window and saw, towering over our heads, a steep, green cliff on which the trees seemed to cling as if standing one on another's heads, we saw the tawny mass of Alphonse

JANAC FROM THE OLD FORTRESS

ON A GREEN GARDEN SEAT

de Poitier's fortress reared against the upper sky, we saw a fringe of houses along the ridge like crenellations on a green fortress. Then the train moved on, thrust us into the darkness of a tunnel, plunged straight through the peninsular hill of Janac and swung us down the deep, green gorges of the Aveyron river.

We got out at the next station and set about inquiring our way back. The map showed two roads, one on each side of the river. That to the east made sixteen kilometres of what was about seven as the crow flies, the other offered you nineteen kilometres but might contain a short cut. So we asked a stolid peasant how we might best come from thence to Janac.

"*Pardi*," he replied, " by the railway."

" But we wish to walk."

"*Pardi*," answered he, " by the railway all the same."

" Is one, then, allowed to walk by the railway ? "

He shrugged his shoulders.

"*Ma foi*," he returned, " one is not *allowed*, but nevertheless one goes that way."

And indeed along the side of the railway a well-trodden path—even marked with the spoor of bicycles—showed that convenience had conquered authority.

The river gorges were deep and fragrant with the full monotonous green of early summer. The sky above the hills showed perhaps an eighth of a full hemisphere, a mere arch instead of a dome ; below our feet the river brawled in its brown bed spotted with boulders. The air was soft with the sunlight and sweet with the acacia ; and, as we went along gaily stepping out beside the rails, we could allow ourselves to wonder how that delicious odour would incorporate into an omelet—for a drover in the train had talked of acacia omelet. I remember as a boy how saddened I would become at my failures to transform the fugitive scent of a flower into an edible flavour, how I pondered over the divergence between the smell and the taste of a violet. Later, in the East, I found strange Chinese liqueurs scented like the gardens of Paradise but as disgusting to the tongue as a chewed violet itself. Was it possible, I now reflected, to make acacia a real flavouring for a table dainty? We have not yet found out.

The railway was lined with acacia trees, and the falling

GANGS OF SPANIARDS.

blossoms had spread in places an almost snowy covering over the metal. There was plenty of room to walk, for the railway, planned once as the principal southern road through France, has been degraded in favour of another line, and the broad embankments, bridges and tunnels designed for a double rail carry but a single line. The rails themselves, to the eye of an ex-engineer, showed that almost universal shabbiness into which France has fallen since the War; some of the rails ought to have been changed long ago. At last are they making reluctant preparations to refurbish the line. Gangs of Spaniards are being recruited; gangs of Spaniards who haunt the Hôtel Sestrol waiting for Raymond, secretary of the Mayor, to inscribe them in his register amongst the more transient inhabitants of Janac.

There were tunnels to walk through, and in these tunnels the side paths were covered with earth and refuse, so that it was no easy matter to keep one's footing as one felt one's way cautiously in the darkness. As soon as the glimmer from the tunnel's mouth had disappeared, as soon as we were in total darkness, all sense of direction faded from the mind. I no longer had a knowledge of how tall I was, my feet seemed at a distance beneath me, at least four yards below. We crept along like blind men exploring with the points of our sticks. In the largest tunnel we were surprised by the passage of a train. We heard it coming; but until it was almost upon us we could not be sure of how far we were from the rails, nor of how far we should be from the rails, since on the other side of us was a deep ditch of sooty water waiting to catch us if we flinched too far. From four yards tall I shrank to a very tiny thing as the huge engine, pistons thrashing, wheels clanking on the degenerate rails, seemed suddenly to fill the whole tunnel with its iron sulphurous bulk.

Out into the blessed sunlight once more, where we found a bed of wild strawberries, on which I feasted double share. Jo had been forbidden strawberries by the doctor, so she had the meagre satisfaction of plucking for her husband to eat.

The railway made ten kilometres of very pleasant walking, at the end of which a sudden bend brought us to a view of Janac fortress from the side opposite to that which we had seen from the train. Here the hill-side was equally steep and barred the route, the railway pointed to the cliff, made a hole in it and went straight through, one could see the light glimmering at the far end of the tunnel; the river turned with a magnificent curve to the left and swept away to encircle the great headland upon which Janac Castle stands, a lighthouse of the dark ages, four hundred feet above the water. From where we were Janac Church, a twelfth-century building, stood just below the castle, seeming to cling to the hillside rather than to be founded on it. To the left of the church a tiny village of crumbling houses—all of the Middle Ages—formed a fit accompaniment to church and castle. The fortress itself looked like the leader of a procession, for from its high hill point, all along a catenary ridge, a long village of huddled houses tailed away for at least a kilometre to a château hidden in trees on a height at the far extremity. Janac village consisted of this one long street, here and there thickening with narrow side alleys, here and there thinning to one opposing row of houses massed high against the sky.

A long, hot climb up the hill-side brought us to the village at last, led us into a cobbled way, which by steep steps zigzagged aloft till we stood in Janac itself. The one main street curved upwards to the castle on the right and upwards again to the main mass of the village on the left. The road was narrow, rough, and plentifully bestrewn with cow's dung; over it the houses leaned inwards, projecting on narrow corbels at the first story. Fill this road with halberdiers and equerries, wenches and scullions and hardly a trace, except the glass in the windows, would warn one that the fifteenth century had not come solidly alive. The village was grey in colour, the meridional sun struck it out in sharp contrasts of light and shade, made the schistine roofs shine with the iridescence of silver except where mosses and lichens had laid their harlequin pattern of green and orange. Under a dimmer sky, beneath a more tempered light, this hoary old village might have been as credible a ghost of the past as any phantom in morion and buckler.

The peasants themselves in their long smocks were not too discordant with the scene, the smock has a respectable antiquity. There seemed, in comparison with the normal villages we had passed through during our walk, a fair amount of bustle about Janac.

"Evidently prosperous," we said to ourselves.

The road was fashioned along the very apex of the ridge. Wherever a gap showed between houses, the grimy alley fell away at once at an angle of forty-five degrees or more, so that a modest hovel with its two stories to the road was a four-storied mansion to the external view. The ridge broadened a little to admit the Gothic basin of a fountain. On the twelve panels of the basin could be discerned rude carvings of heads and a raised inscription half effaced; which the natives devoutly believe to be in Hebrew, but has been deciphered into nothing more important than a record of the names of the Seigneurs who erected this strange relic of the past. Over this ponderous Gothic remain an urn fashioned in cement spouted three thin trickles of water beneath which the copper buckets were standing.

We came to our triangular place. Here we hesitated in doubt. We were eager for lunch, but having traversed some length of village without perceiving inn or restaurant we had begun to wonder whether we were to go hungry.

Here came an official. He wore the French official cap, his hair was grey and rather long beneath it, his blouse was blue with embroidered letters on the collar, he carried a side drum, the drumsticks stuck into a leather belt.

In answer to our query he waved a hand to the apex of our triangle.

"Eat there if you like," he said.

"There?" we exclaimed.

"Food's good there," he answered gruffly. "Yet, if you don't like it, there are hotels higher up."

And he continued his way downhill.

Our query—"There?"—which had appeared to irritate the *garde champêtre*, had been drawn from us by astonishment, not, as he had imagined, by disdain. The place appeared to be a hat and clothier's shop. One window which bordered the open door was filled with hats, another window, before which was set a table, spilled out an assortment of cloths and cottons, while on the table itself stood a headless mannequin in a cotton dress, which waved its empty arms in the faint breeze with the absurd caricature of a politician making a speech. Very pompous and portentous did that figure look and its gestures were most significant. They were as though the welfare of France depended upon that mannequin being returned top of the polls. We did not at once perceive the connection between a hat shop and lunch.

However, we stooped to the dark doorway and came inside a sombre room; figures in black blouses occupied the tables, faces darkened by the sun scrutinized us, mastication was almost vocal, a woman, twin sister of the mannequin, but this time with a head, accosted us. Could we lunch? Certainly. Outside in the fresh air? If we liked. How much did it cost? Six francs each with wine and coffee. The place was crowded, all these peasants were indulging in meals at six francs apiece.

At a table, set outside the door, we sat down, our appetites sharpened by the odour from the kitchen. The sister of the mannequin brought out half of a huge loaf the shape of a penny bun, and holding it beneath her chin as though it were a violin she bowed us off two generous slabs of bread.

MAIN STREET OF JANAC

Then came a bottle of red wine, an urn of soup heavy with bread crusts, *lapin chasseur* (not *chassé*, though, for the rabbits are tame), fresh peas, veal cutlets, custard, wild strawberries and biscuits, coffee and cognac. Each time that the waitress brought us a new dish we were more impressed by her resemblance to the mannequin, except of course the head, though there too the resemblance went further than we could at the moment suspect as the waitress did for a time *lose her head*, as the saying is. She was in an asylum for several years. When the meal was about half finished, Madame Sestrol herself came to the door, and smilingly demanded if the food were delectable. We gesticulated our enthusiasm.

" Janac is lively," we said.

" But it is market day," she answered, waving her hand down the road.

The market-place of Janac has been contrived by the simple device of roofing over a part of the road. Here were grouped a few peasants, one or two women with baskets full of chickens, and one or two egg merchants who were packing their morning purchases into crates. We had thought Janac bustling for a normal village, but had to confess to ourselves that it was empty for a market day.

***

Janac market does not belie its appearance. It is a moribund affair. The Mayor and corporation are now trying artificial respiration. Notices printed on pink paper announce the opening of the autumn fairs. Owners of pigs and calves are exhorted to do their utmost to stimulate trade ; we are promised large influxes of well-known cattle dealers. Moreover, bribes are offered, the seller of a calf receives two francs bounty, the carter who brought the calf to market is also subsidized ; pigs too are *assisted :* but in a less generous manner, though two francs only represents about threepence in our money.

At one time Janac was a metropolis. Anciently it was the seat of the Seneschal of the province, and the architecture of the crumbling cottages around the fortress bears traces of bygone magnificence. But the ideal town of the days of the arquebus is a nuisance in those of the autobus. To-day it is fatiguing to drive one's calves up four hundred feet of precipitous ascent when all about the countryside there are markets and fairs more easily approachable.

Mechanical transport has strangled Janac fair. Before the railway came the peasants had little idea of saving time, they would have agreed with Arnold that the train which took one quickly " from a dismal and illiberal life in Islington to a dismal and illiberal life in Camberwell " was little advance in civilization. If he possessed a speedy horse, what the farmer enjoyed was the prowess of his animal and the poetry of motion. Janac fair in spite of its elevation remained a function. But the railway and later the motor-car has infected everybody with the disease of useless speed. Indeed, for the poor man an advance in the speed of transport is a real tragedy, for the act of travelling is a poor man's holiday, and the slower it is the longer the holiday. The train too has brought outside, impatient cattle speculators. During the course of the War a bullock would often change hands eight or ten times in an afternoon. These cattle speculators are shy of Janac, the roads are too long, those marks as of embroidery on the map have no charm for the modern drover.

So within the remembrance of the present generation Janac fair has dwindled till it is at the point of extinction. A French Mayor does not offer bonuses till things are in a desperate condition. The offer of a bonus is the proof of the pudding. But it is typical of the French peasant that he will spend money trying to revive a dying market with threepenny bonuses, while he will not enlarge his village reservoir, thus starving the populace for a whole month by the lack of water. Nor will he make Janac a happy hunting-ground for summer visitors. The railway has brought fifteenth-century Janac abruptly in face with the twentieth century. She has not yet recognized that she is a picturesque ruin.

**

Only one person has recognized what a ruin is Janac, and, moreover, how to gather advantage nowadays from a ruin. This man is the doctor, Monsieur Saggebou. He has been urging on the villagers the necessity of transforming the village into a " centre du Tourism." He goes round preaching the hotel and the lodging house with vociferous persistence. He is thick set, bearded, untidy and limping. He prefers to do his doctoring in the middle of the street where he lectures the passers-by as though he were a professor in a hospital. A boy with a broken ankle was brought in a cart. The doctor set his leg at the door of the Hôtel Sestrol. He mouthed medical terms with gusto to an uncomprehending audience, tibia, fibula, tendon Achilles, peroneus, gastroenemius, soleus, extensor longus digitorum, tibialis anticus and other words of magic properties mystified the tymphanum of the peasant. The boy yelled like blue murder, but the doctor was enjoying himself. He explained to everybody what a wonderful doctor he was, and what a mess any other man would have made of this particular fracture. He lectures us upon the incontestable superiority of France to all other lands, in people, food, climate and learning, and he has told us many strange things we did not know about England, to which country he has never travelled.

The doctor's idea of turning Janac into a show village is feasible, it may be the sole method of drawing profit from her decadence. But, alas, the doctor has talked so much, has declaimed so persistently that the very fact of his

THE BROKEN LEG.

championing is almost enough to set the populace against the idea. He now aims his discourse chiefly at Sestrol. The latter is *débrouillard*, devoid of fog, a clear-sighted person; but Sestrol shakes his head with a grin. His adventurous days are over; he is now content to rest with what he has done, which is well enough.

*_**

But let us come back to our first lunch at Janac.

The excellence of the *lapin chasseur* tempted Jo to ask from the waitress-mannequin whether lodgings were to be found in Janac. It was an arrow apparently shot into the air, but aimed, of course, at the Hôtel Sestrol. As those negro tribes will place a mark flat on the ground ten feet from their stance and shooting an arrow almost perpendicularly will pierce the target, so Jo fired at the Hôtel Sestrol with a casual demand. In dealing with peasants such caution is often advisable. A direct demand they will dodge as a nigger foe will dodge a straightly fired arrow. The idea must be given time as an abstraction, to concrete itself gradually. The waitress passed our question on to Madame Sestrol. Madame Sestrol answered that in the faubourg, at the top of the hill, was an hotel, the Hôtel Quemac, where we would, as the season was yet early, doubtless find accommodation.

However, coffee brought out to us a small man bowed beneath a panama hat. Making allowances for difference of tint between ebony and meridional flesh his face might have been carved by a negro sculptor, there were the highly arched eyebrows, moulding into the thin, overlong straight nose like a column and a pair of vaults, bulbous eyes, a straight mouth set in a protuberant upper lip, high cheekbones and cadaverous jaw. Do not think that Monsieur Sestrol is in the least like a negro, he is like that variety of negro art which is so curious because it has nothing of the negro in it. As he placed our coffee in tall glasses on the table he begged the favour of being allowed to drink his own coffee in our company. He had a humorous twinkle in his eye, a sub-sardonic kind of illumination, but we surprised him with a résumé of our travels afoot, we interested him with hasty generalizations about the favourite *bête noire* of Southern France—at once *bête noire* and drudge —the Spaniard. France is short of " *la main d'œuvre* "; Spain is short of " *le pognon,*" respectively " the hand of toil " and the " fist full of cash," so they mutually exchange labour and lucre, neither one becoming the more content with the other in process. The Spaniard dislikes and (being usually stupid) despises his master; the Frenchman distrusts and fears his hind. Much of the bad blood is, of course, bred only by differences of cooking and of language. The Spaniard who remains long enough in France to learn French often shows a reluctance to go back to his native country. Indeed, in Spain itself they say, " Distrust a Spaniard who speaks French," which indicates that out of the shoals of Spaniards who cross the frontier northwards only those return to Spain who are too stupid to learn French, or who are too vicious to be easy under the eye of the French police.

A twenty-five centime cigar and the cognac in his coffee put Monsieur Sestrol into such a good humour that he said :

" We have, for instance, a room over our stable. You might be inclined to look at it, without committing yourselves."

He went into the hotel where we heard later that the following dialogue ensued :

Monsieur Sestrol : " Maria, where are the keys of the *remise ?* I'm going to show the rooms to the strangers."

Madame Sestrol : " To the strangers ? Then, do you know them ? "

Monsieur Sestrol : " Not the least in the world."

Madame Sestrol : " But we cannot let to foreigners whom we know not at all."

Monsieur Sestrol : " *Pardi*, no. Not in general, I admit. But these people amuse me."

He led us down the road, past the row of old grey stone houses, past the mad priest's, past the aristocratic shoemaker, past the café and the forge, beneath the hangar of the market, where four mournful blackly dressed peasant women still were nursing unsold hens, past the paper-shop to the three-storied primitive box of a house—three-quarters buried in the hill—on the front of which a board painted in faded lettering announced, REMISE, HÔTEL SESTROL.

We soon finished our inspection and came tactfully to the price.

"Hum," replied Monsieur Sestrol, communing with himself, "without an exact committal, shall we suggest ten francs a day? But of course you won't get market-day meals all the time. Eat as we eat, *hein?*"

* *
*

The "Hôtel" Sestrol indeed was pretentious only in title. It had a cheap letter-paper with the title printed upon it. To the balcony over the front door a signboard was fixed with the same misleading inscription; but the acacia trees planted when Monsieur Saggebou was Mayor have covered over this misleading signboard. The hotel was part drinking shop, part country restaurant, part hat shop and part general drapers. It had, indeed, reversed the practice of our greater emporiums where the restaurant is an addendum, a convenience for customers where feeding is a luxury incidental to the duty of shopping. Here the shop was but an annex to the restaurant, shopping being a luxury added to the necessity of dining.

For casual voyagers the "Hôtel" had never a room to spare. Those over the stable which we had accepted "without committal" had for years been occupied by the "contrairy" lodger, and in the house itself the total chambers of the upper floor numbered but four. One was a trying-on room, general store, etc., for the shop, one was a mere cupboard where slept Élise, one was the bedroom of Monsieur and Madame, one was the drawing-room in which Raymond slept on a couch. They were all in a straight line opening into one another except the cupboard of Élise, for family privacy is a luxury which seems to have developed in regions north of latitude 45°.

So that as an hotel, the restaurant-hatshop-drapers, Sestrol may be considered a fraud. With the exercise of persuasion, a belated farmer or a well-known commercial traveller might get the privilege of sleeping with Raymond, but there was the limit of the hotel's capacity. Before Élise came they had once let the cupboard to a young couple, who arriving one rainy night had played upon their compassion, but this relaxation of rules was ill repaid. The police descended upon the hotel, the young man having abducted the girl, a wealthy and infatuated minor. During the escapade, which had lasted a month, the young adventurers had made a living by hawking fraudulent face powders and false cures for eczema to the ignorant peasantry.

We got our rooms over the stable by pure chance. Madame Sestrol had objected to us merely as strangers; Monsieur Sestrol had accepted us in dictation to a whim, for he was a man who prided himself on possessing *flair*. We were accepted in reality because I was wearing trousers; or rather because I was not wearing knickerbockers. On walking tours I generally clothe myself in the latter, but on this day some good spirit had chosen my garments. No whim of Monsieur Sestrol could have battled against the knickerbocker. To Janac knickerbockers have but one signification, they are as terrible as were blue stockings to the Victorian. To Janac the knickerbocker is Bolshevik.

An anarchist from Carmaux once made a speech in Janac. He wore knickerbockers and by the use of the syllogistic method which has proved Socrates human Janac henceforth knows the knickerbocker to be as deadly a signal as the Jolly Roger.

*_**

The market day *was* in truth almost a nonentity. In the blacksmith's café, an accordion player was squashing out metallic melody to which five men and seven girls were dancing. After each dance the men dropped their partners on to a bench and went back to the tables where they had left their drinks. We sipped a coffee for a while, watching this temperate amusement. Then with a salute to the company we went out to make further explorations.

Above the triangular place the street sloped yet more steeply, so steeply indeed that to get from the upper village to the lower the carts generally make a wide detour. Here the houses had balconies which were draped in vine, but the same hand of age had mellowed all the contours; no comfortable modernity disturbed this dream of the past.

In their appreciation of beauty the peasants and villagers are no whit in advance of their buildings. The sentiment for the picturesque is of recent birth. Little over a hundred years ago, Chateaubriand, placing his tragic Atala in the primitive forests of America, was accused of having produced an *ugly* thing. The primitive forest, known to be wild, unsympathetic, was therefore *ugly*; one could find no comfort there, it was ugly. So in many things to-day we still associate beauty with physical desirability. The woman we would wish to embrace is beautiful. Janac, picturesque Janac, is ugly to its possessors. But it shows the refinement of the normal French mind that the peasant will say: "C'est pittoresque, oui; mais ce n'est pas beau."

Yet it is difficult to see how the blindest could deny the *beauty* of Janac, when one comes suddenly, over the crest of the steep and narrow street, into the broad Place du Grifoules,* the centre of the faubourg. An open *place*, broad and long, centred by a double line of young acacia trees under which a few desolate cattle stood, making the pretence of being a fair. On one side of the long *place*, the houses lean out on the upper story, resting upon shaky-looking columns of grey stone, forming thus a long, deep, covered walk under the shadow of which lurk village shops and peasant crafts, the waggon builder, the blacksmith of the faubourg, the atheist cobbler, the tinsmith and so on. These houses with high peaked roofs, with floors sagging overhead, with crumbling plaster and oblique windows, seem fit places of conspiracy, suitable refuges for the Croquants, the peasants of Limousin, of Agenais and of Quercy who, revolting against the Crown in 1594, made Janac one of the headquarters of revolt. But the Place du Grifoules can scarcely claim so remote a date as the sixteenth century. At that time Janac must have clustered timorously near the castle walls, a-shiver round the warmth of refuge and for ever feeling the chill of danger at its back. Yet time has cured any apparent differences of age in Janac, what was new in the seventeenth century is old now, and all has one-time scarred face—so you can perceive few differences between two sisters, one of ninety and one of eighty, though the one may have dandled the other.

The Place du Grifoules leads into another *place* covered with burned grass, an irregular space about as big as a croquet lawn. Here stand two *beautiful* houses, that of the chemist, and that of Janac's second doctor. These houses

* Grifoules, brass griffin head for water fountain, a common name for southern village squares.

THE ROAD WHICH CONTOURS JANAC MILL

ON A GREEN GARDEN SEAT

are the last word in commonplace architecture, but they are modern: the peasant sees them *not* with the eye of the æsthetic. Does he in fact *see* at all? His beauty is sensational, sentimental rather, to use the word in its proper meaning.

A road led us downhill, swung round a corner, dropped between vineyards in curves along the side of the hill and at last brought us back to our own *remise*, and so past blacksmith, shoemaker, mad priest and Tuk-Tuk to the hospitable Hôtel Sestrol, where we made arrangements to return at once to Janac.

We took our way back through the long village street, down the other side of Janac promontory, four hundred feet of descent to the station perched by the brown waters of the Aveyron, opposite to a fine old mill built in the beautiful architecture of the French château style.

III

MINE HOST AND HOSTESS OF THE HÔTEL SESTROL

The Sestrols

A HUMAN being may be likened to a geographical island, in that he is a solid body bounded by oceans of a more fluid substance, and that his peninsulars, the arms and legs, do project downwards in the proper geographical fashion. But there are times, under the persuasion of a suitably summered heat, when man, gently annealed—not roasted—seems to lose his boundaries and to merge, slumbrously and content, with the illimitable universe. From such a moment, on the green garden seat where we have been dozing and reflecting for an hour, we are aroused by the quick march of Monsieur Sestrol swinging up the road. Monsieur Sestrol is almost a dwarf and almost hunchbacked; his face we have described; his arms hang bowed, his hands are curved like iron links which have drawn open, his clothes and boots are countrified, but he wears a real panama hat, at a rakish angle. The great part of the farmers about Janac thus wear panamas, the only indications of the general prosperity which the war has disseminated over the country-side. Indeed, the peasant, while quite aware that he ought to hate the Germans and deplore the war, finds it almost impossible to do so with any sincerity. If he has not lost a son, all he knows of the war is that he was formerly indebted, with worn-out implements, with profits not large enough to pay his way when war broke out; now he finds himself freed from anxiety, with money in the bank, with new tools and with prices so high that he can afford to give his superfluous milk and eggs to the pigs, if not offered what he considers good money for them. But in outward appearance he has changed little, his wife still is huddled into her black bombazine, his daughters look like neophytes of Charlie Chaplin about the feet, he wears his black blouse. Only the panama hat betrays his prosperity.

Sestrol has walked his fifteen kilometres before breakfast. He is no more exempt than the generality of villagers from a variety of trades. He began life as a herdsboy. He states that his first labour was undertaken at the age of four, when he was commanded to look after a dog which was looking after sheep, and he ascribes his stunted growth to early hardship and to childish toil. Yet early toil seems to have done little to deteriorate the energy of his frame. He is never tired. Here he comes swinging in from his fifteen kilometres fresh as a daisy. To-day he will work continuously till six or seven. Fourteen hours is nothing to him. He comes in from a country round with his pockets full of money, like the sailor in the old song. He has been collecting advances, mortgages, interests due to a Francheville bank, of which he is the local agent.

His career has developed thus: from herdsboy to tailor's

apprentice, from tailor's apprentice to tailor (no typical tailor he, but rather like the valiant little tailor of Hans Andersen), from tailor to mail-carrier, from mail-carrier to bricklayer, from bricklayer to hatter and *modiste* and draper, from draper to innkeeper, from innkeeper to bank agent, from bank agent to landowner. Sestrol is an example of the ascending current of peasantry. His son Raymond has been educated, went to college in Albi, and is now the Mayor's secretary, village fireman, and, to his parents' disgust, unreclaimed Benedick.

* * *

Monsieur Sestrol is faintly jealous of our career. Wanderings in Spain, walking tours in Southern Slavia, holidays upon the Adriatic and so on. He looks upon us as an infringement of his prerogative. He counts that his life is the most interesting that ever was lived, and has said over the coffee glasses:

"You could write a most extraordinary romance of my life, if you knew it all."

When I uttered the platitude that every man's life is a romance, he retorted:

"Not such as mine has been. Mine has been *so* adventurous."

One wonders, perhaps, what adventures could arrive within the very circumscribed limit of his wanderings, which fifteen miles either side of Janac would surely enclose, all but a very few sallies. But his idea of adventurous is better expressed by the word "hard." And doubtless from this angle he had had a most "adventurous" life. One day recently he was discovered by Raymond sitting in a ditch on the road to St. André in company with the father-in-law of the *épicier*-cobbler. Each was in tears, for each, having boasted of the duress of his past, had called to mind so many pathetic memories that self pity had " whelmed him o'er," and the rivalry of hardship had ended in a brotherhood of tears.

Sestrol has, indeed, been treated harshly, but not indignantly by fate, but he counts himself a mark for ill fortune, from the age of two years. He tells the story in a truly peasant fashion; or is it not a profoundly natural fashion to pile up all the details leading to the tragedy and then merely to indicate the tragedy itself? He tells you the age of the nursemaid, the locality, a description of the sow, of the stable entry, of the kind of particular flower, a daisy, which the nurse was chewing at the moment, and of the kind of whistling noise she was making with her teeth, all these minutely catalogued; but the main incident, how the nursemaid came to tread on the sow's back, how the sow uprising in a flurry projected nurse and baby in arms into the stable, how the weight of the nurse fell upon the baby and so on, are all left vague to such an extent that it is merely by conjunction of *dramatis personæ* with result that subsequently the story becomes coherent in the mind. The result is that Monsieur Sestrol cannot sneeze. Never has that insidious tickle invaded his nose, never has that exhilarant inflation spread his chest, never has that devastating climax, " A-tish-oo ! " sent the blood tingling and leaping in his veins.

But it is thus with all of Sestrol's stories. The account of Sestrol's snowing up is full of circumstantial detail until the moment when it is most expected. He will begin with how as a lad of fourteen, apprentice tailor, he gambled away two months' money, no lack here of circumstance. How he gambled away all that he had in his pocket; how the master tailor, a partner in the game, advanced him a first month's pay in order to recoup his losses; the disappearance of this paltry sum also; his hesitancies; his calculations; the persuasion of his fellows; the cheery optimism of the master tailor; the advance of a second sum; the loss of that too; his destitution—Sestrol will give you all of these with fidelity. The advent of Christmas; determination to spend the holiday at home, albeit bearing no gifts; the

SESTROL'S SNOWING UP.

resolution to trudge the path, twelve miles or so, since no money remained to take diligence; the beginning of the storm; the increasing difficulty of walking; the lost way—facts are still definite though the particularization becomes vaguer. But of the desperate affair itself, of how the lad Sestrol was buried up to the neck, of how he was becoming frozen, of his cries, of the woman who heard them through the lull of the storm and who came pluckily to his rescue, and of how he lay a fortnight in bed he will make but the vaguest sketch, only totally intelligible after several repetitions. He can give the clearest picture of his feelings over the loss of two months' wages, but of that of being frozen to death not a line.

This is an instinct in the primitive nature, ornament is perfected before melody, the description of costume before that of character. The manner of a man's death is less circumstantial than the manner of his clothes; and perhaps this is correctly proportioned. If you can visualize a man externally you can lend him enough of your common humanity to accompany him into oblivion, death comes alike to all; it is dress which can be individual. That is the quality of simple yarns. All the details until the exciting moment and then a summary of one line. Yet the thing is so full of circumstance that we make it live of our own accord. On the contrary, in many a modern writer we may often feel that it is the death agony of a ghost which is being so elaborately enacted.

Sestrol's belief in the adventurous nature of his past is largely vague general reminiscence. He has climbed from being a poor herdsboy to becoming a landowner, is not that in itself conclusive of adventure? Pressed for details he is apt to lack incident. Poverty, hardship and hard work would not seem to most of us to be adventurous unless we are contemplating the hardships of some one else; starvation is only romance when 'tis another who is starving.

Sestrol's next positive adventure comes with his courtship. By this time he was a journeyman tailor at Francheville, and he met Madame Sestrol at a country fête. She was a village girl living some four miles from Janac, a trouser maker by trade. We do not hear that her *dangerous* profession laid her open to the temptations under which the girl depicted by Sterne so lucklessly succumbed, seduced by her *métier*. But maybe no squire's son, evilly intentioned, came making an insidious court through her trade. At any rate she had resisted the advances of a burly village companion, frowned upon by her family, since he was what the village called " a bad character." Sestrol, honest tradesman, was encouraged by the parents as a makeweight against the undesirable, and Marie herself, with a strange combination of French characteristics, passion and calculation, soon perceived that the greater chance of success lay by the side of the steady Sestrol than on that of the more irregular, though probably more attractive, suitor. Happiness? I wonder if she gave happiness a thought? Rather she drove forward as do so many of us under the impulse of a fear of the future. We who talk about humanity's aim, do we stop to think whether humanity can have an aim? We may be surging forward, but isn't our urge rather a rush, a panic race from starvation? Is it possible that persons who are merely fleeing blindly from terror can be held to *have* an aim?

About two and a half miles from Janac there is a sharp curve in the road, and here one night, returning from his courtship, Sestrol had what he describes as the biggest fright of his life. His discomfited rival had threatened to do him an injury. Coming to this bend on his homeward route Sestrol perceived in the darkness a large figure which seemed to be waiting for him. Sestrol, very much alarmed, dodged into the hedge hoping that he had been unheard, for he was wearing the string-soled shoes of the country, but his opponent followed his example. So for a while they both crouched, Sestrol trying to estimate the probable manœuvres of his enemy. Like the old tale tellers, he is not frightened of fear; he has no false shame; he does not hesitate to admit that he was sweating with terror. After a time, he reflected that a small man with a large stone might be a match for a bigger opponent, and set about arming himself with road metal. Then he decided that in the hedge he might be taken at a disadvantage, and

THE SCARE.

so he stepped back into the open road, to invite an attack, to have done with suspense.

From the hedge a quavering voice inquired:

"Isn't that Sestrol?"

"It is," replied the now valiant little tailor.

"God be praised. I thought you were a robber," exclaimed his future brother-in-law emerging in his turn.

They shook hands, kissed one another on both cheeks and went each his way; each for the moment a little more positively alive, each for a precious ten minutes a man-and-a-half in value.

Sestrol is not quite a peasant of the fictional type. He is not parsimonious, though he has a proper French respect for money; he is a freethinker though he is superstitious; a faithful husband, who loves a sexual suggestion or a crude joke; a man with a serious aim in life who despises a solemn fellow.

He has a sub-acid humour which loves to exercise itself upon a village know-all; and he invents a variety of tricks to ridicule that kind of a fellow. A typical example of his satire is the following.

The village is lit by electricity from an old mill converted into a dynamo house. The proprietor who does most of his own work lives in the village and superintends the light, but must keep a mechanic, resident in the mill itself four hundred feet below in the river-bed. He was on the point of engaging a new assistant; and the new man had in some way aroused Sestrol's antagonism. So the evening after the change had been effected Sestrol stopped the new mechanic in the village street.

"Hey, Charles," he cried, "I've got something for you. Albert, before he went away, told me on no account to forget to hand it to you, it's an important part of the machinery down there."

And he passed to Charles a piece of metal.

Charles turned it over in his hand. He could not, of course, in one day be perfectly acquainted with the machine under his charge, but he was also reluctant to admit to Sestrol that he did not recognize the piece. So he said with false gratitude:

"Ah, yes, thank you very much. I know exactly where that fits. I don't know what we would have done without it. I am glad that Albert didn't forget to leave it."

Sestrol went off chuckling. He had given to Charles a pig's nose-ring.

Janac exports chestnuts, plums and walnuts to England. In the little village station the casual traveller is surprised to find large piles of the characteristic baskets from Covent Garden stacked for transport. Janac can understand why so much fruit should be sent to England. It has learned

IN THE RIVER-BED.

from Dr. Saggebou that the English climate is so foggy and raw that fruit will not ripen in these islands. But one importation puzzles Janac, that of mistletoe.

What can the English want with mistletoe?

For many years the village was satisfied with the solution that the English made mistletoe into jam. During the war strangers from the north, fugitives, came to Janac and made into jam the blackberry, which is reputed to be poisonous, so why should not the English make mistletoe jam. But a village know-all arose who squashed this absurd idea. Mistletoe jam indeed, pooh! Why, everybody knows that the mistletoe is a most important factor in the English Church services at Christmas, they are heretics and they ascribe to the mistletoe magic virtues. We concluded that some hint of Druidical rites must have drifted to him. Sestrol was delighted to learn the true use of mistletoe, delighted yet puzzled. He was delighted to be able to taunt the know-all, but puzzled at the queer foolishness of the English. To import at such expense a frivolous, useless vegetable which might give an excuse for a sly kiss or two—nonsense! Incredible! People don't do such things! Reason and evidence fought a battle in him. His capitulation being expressed in the usual terms—" *Chacun ses idées, quoi ?* "

This is his favourite method of defence against us, "*Chacun ses idées, chacun son métier.*" He likes us undoubtedly, but he finds us know-alls who are difficult to catch out. Our slender stock of facts, our tit-bit accumulations do almost adequately cover the field of possible query on the part of Sestrol, except in his own craft of which we are careful to profess ignorance. So that when his tentative inquiries let loose upon him a flood of undesired information—we are, I fear, somewhat eager Apostles—he battles against the intrusion of the unknown with his defensive phrase. He remains content to know that we know, or that we appear to know. It is, of course, rather unfortunate for him. He asks questions which on the surface are simple enough, about painting, for example, but the normal activities of civilized man are so complex nowadays that any of our answers whirl him off to what is practically a fourth dimension for him, Einstein is no more incredible to a peasant than a street full of picture galleries, the Rue la Boetie. So that he is continually forced to fight us off with his "*Chacun son métier*."

Yet this phrase must be admitted as a broadminded admission. Your English yokel does not admit so much; he says, "It's better'n doin' nowt," or words to that effect. So your French peasant in his heart may consider one a fainéant, but there is a difference. Fainéant means a man who survives without labour, whom the French peasant in his heart despises but whom the English yokel would admire. In England the artist is despised not because he doesn't work but because he *does* work.

* * *

Sestrol's marriage installed him in Janac as tailor with his wife as trouser maker. She was a plump and a good girl to look at in those days, I'm sure. But they hadn't a penny between them. Their marriage will have been an ordinary Janac wedding, a tradition which is dying out. We saw a modern wedding in which the parties straggled in a group to the Mairie, with a studied unconventionality which annoyed the villagers very much. "I don't know what marriages are coming to nowadays," grumbled Madame Sestrol.

In *her* time they went in a prim procession with music, first to the Mairie for the civil or legal ceremony, thence to the church for the religious or emotional consummation; then home again to the feasting and fleshly rites. Another Janac tradition is dying out, a queer old custom of an embarrassing nature. The bride and bridegroom's first bedding was treated as a sort of hide-and-seek affair. They had to slip away from the half-drunken guests, to find some private corner in which to enjoy their first intimacies. As soon as their absence was marked, a halloo and cry was set up after them, and could they be discovered a new feast was begun around their couch, however unconventional it might be.

Sestrol never told us how he avoided his pursuers, but knowing the man I am prepared to bet that he did; he would invent some wily ruse to save his new wife from blushes.*

They supplemented their earnings by carrying the mail. From the station in the deep valley up to the post-office at the far end of the town is no mean climb, five hundred feet nearly, but husband and wife shared the labour. He carried the heavy bag from the station up to their house below the castle walls, she bore it up the less precipitous length of the village. I forget what trivial sum this hard labour earned them: only I know this, that having toiled so for many years I would hardly dare to call it *adventure*.

With the earnings thus slowly accumulated they bought the plot of land on which the Hôtel Sestrol now stands. It is a narrow angular piece, on which was built an old barn, at the back was a garden belonging to another proprietor. Sestrol turned bricklayer. He set to work in his spare time and destroyed the old barn, upon it erecting the new house, with the help of his wife and a workman. They were very annoyed with the proprietor of the garden behind who refused to give permission to make windows at the back of the house. It seems that this is one of the property perquisites of France, but the reason of refusal is not for privacy, the man did not fear to be overlooked, but he feared that

---

* Though the weddings have lost character the funerals still retain one curious custom. Early in the procession is carried a spread-out piece of cloth held stretched by the corners, the bearers being the nearest neighbours of the dead. For old persons the sheet is black, for the young it is white with a maltees cross of laurel leaves stitched upon the cloth.

the Sestrols would throw their slops and rubbish out of the window on to his garden.

Sestrol's character is exhibited by the fact that his was the first hat shop in Janac. Hat sellers travel round to every country fair, but a hat shop in a village had not been

HAT BOOTH IN A COUNTRY FAIR.

thought of; and at first Sestrol himself had also toured hats to the neighbouring villages on fair days. A village enterprise has only to be moderately successful to find imitators. Because one hat shop contrives a living, three or four envious competitors spring into being so that the lauded benefits of competition reduce all competitors to starvation. From this arises the multiplicity of village enterprise. The small profit on hats has to be augmented with sales of tobacco, or of sweets, or of underlinen, so that instead of twenty shops each selling its speciality you have twenty shops each selling samples of twenty different trades. Away goes the power of keeping reserve stocks, away goes selection, away goes quality.

The Sestrols, however, did a clever and unusual thing, they made the hat and cloth shop an addendum to a restaurant. One eats, one is in a good humour, one is tempted to buy.

No, Sestrol is not an ordinary village character.

Madame Sestrol is not so unusual a person. She would not have taken us in as guests, nor does she ever by the incautious question tiptoe to the edge of the unknown as Sestrol does so frequently. Indeed, to make her understand quite a simple remark requires a certain technique. Jo has a method of introducing a conversation which is like walking into a company backwards: the Henry James style of clarity. This method, which amuses some of our friends, is apt to puzzle those who like to think as if on ruled paper. Sestrol jumps to her meaning quite often; Madame Sestrol is always left floundering in puzzlement, ejaculates " *oui* " and runs away.

For instance, Jo might begin thus:

" Since everybody else tends to keep the black ones, I would always choose a tabby in order to restore the proper balance of colour."

I, casting an eye upon the cat's swollen form, would pick up the reference. But to poor Madame Sestrol, having no clue, the words are mere gibberish. Even if one said positively, "The cat is going to have kittens," she would misunderstand, because at that moment her mind might be running upon ducks, or on hats, or on the kitchen. For one wild moment she would try to force your remark into something pertinent to the subject at that time in her mind; failing, she would give it up. To begin with, one had to switch her on to the main line of thought before running ahead. Thus:

Myself (with emphasis) : " The cat ! "
Madame Sestrol : " Eh ? "
Myself : " The cat."
Madame Sestrol : " What did you say ? "
Myself : " The cat."
Madame Sestrol : " Eh, yes. The cat, certainly ! "
Myself : " The cat is going to have kittens."
Madame Sestrol : " It is perfectly true, monsieur. She bears with great regularity ! "

I pursued these tactics with Madame Sestrol whenever I could remember to do so, with the result that, in spite of the fact that I don't speak French half as well as Jo, the good lady always maintained my superiority in the tongue in contradiction to her husband's more just estimate.

It would appear that the unexercised mind becomes case hardened against new impressions at about the age of sixteen or seventeen. Sestrol is an exception, Madame Sestrol a rigorous example. I would be prepared to bet that making trousers was the last thing that her mind absorbed except, maybe, a few unavoidable facts about marriage and bearing children. She still is intellectually a girl of sixteen. Say that she is now fifty-five one wonders how she can have passed some thirty-nine years surrounded by the infinite gradations of a developing universe and remained

impenetrable. Day after day she would ask us the same question, and after six weeks would be no wiser than on the first day. Aeroplanes and motor-cars she has accepted as facts, but I think that if aeroplanes and motors were forbidden by law, in three years Madame Sestrol would have forgotten that they ever existed.

Yet for all this mental inertia Madame Sestrol is an almost perfect instrument for her place. The restaurant kitchen, buying and selling hats, feeding ducks and stuffing them with maize to give them liver disease, curing hams (Janac hams are mentioned by Rabelais in Gargantua's birth feast) and hunting nettles constitute her daily round. What need has she for absorbing external ideas.

* * *

When we first came to Janac Madame Sestrol aired her chief grievance. She said:

"Now, *monsieur et dame*, you must get me an English girl to marry to my son Raymond."

Raymond is twenty-four, without a wife; his celibacy is a tormenting thought to the father and mother. They are tormented by the idea either of his remaining unmarried or of his choosing a wife who won't work.

"The girl of to-day," sneered Madame Sestrol, "she doesn't want to work. She wants clothes and stockings, *la la*, and high-heeled shoes and underlinen. She wants to walk about like a lady."

The Sestrols grumble at the present generation as their fathers grumbled at the Sestrols, and as the grandfathers grumbled at the fathers, and so on until you can hear old father Adam and mother Eve start the progression with Cain.

They have chosen out suitable lasses, on approval, as it were, for Raymond's bride; but Raymond continues his ungrateful celibacy. One day he dug me in the ribs and pointed to a farmer's daughter who was passing.

"That's a girl they wanted me to marry," he said.

She was a typical farmer's daughter, dressed in that curious ungainly silk uniform which is the general result of the disappearance of local costume. Women's dress is supposed to be adapted to charm, but can anything more ugly be pictured than the average farmer's wife or daughter in ceremonious attire? A man's clothes seldom degenerate into ugliness by simplicity, a farmer is clad, a peasant is often more beautiful in his careless neglect. But was anything invented more conducive to race suicide than the costume of the peasant's wife? And yet these women years ago evolved the beautiful local costumes so suitable to their type. One or two aged women still wear their dignified dresses: old frumps, the farmers' grotesque wives call them probably. This girl might have had some charm had she not been ill fitted everywhere, and laced into stays which made ridges and humps at strange places on her protesting form.

A second of Raymond's fiancées on trial went more picturesquely and sensibly clad in a broad country hat and an overall. A jolly girl, hard working, for ever setting off to the fields with her ox cart or returning laden at night; a rich girl, too, with 40,000 francs dowry. But Raymond would have none of her; she was taboo in the village. Janac cannot boast of more than eight or nine hundred inhabitants for all its length without breadth. Yet she boasts of two doctors, two schools, two lawyers, a tax collector and a chemist. The older lawyer lives in the lower village (our village) just over against the convent and next door to the house where Raymond's rejected lives with her mother and sister. This lawyer was a curious-looking man who seemed as though his soul were too small for him, as though the inside of him were shrunk so that his skin was too large for his body and his clothes too large for his frame, and both skin and clothes had fallen into baggy folds. He stalks the village streets, silent and alone, as the dusk falls. He is a man credited with many conquests, which only increases one's wonder at woman's taste; his sobriquet, "double comb," indicating that Chanticler had but a half of his virility. This old and, apparently, almost friendless roué has fallen into a habit of sitting nightly with the mother and the two girls in their kitchen. He is accused of no wrong intention, yet this simple fact, his mere presence, is enough to scare away all the village youths from what seemed to us the most attractive girls of the place.

Ungrateful celibacy: Madame Sestrol argued thus. For twenty-four years we have toiled and moiled to make Raymond comfortable, not counting the time we laboured before he was born and of which he will in the future reap the advantage. We are old, we wish to lean back upon our son, it is time that Raymond takes a wife who will be servant to our wants. Madame Sestrol considers it unfilial ingratitude that he has refused to provide them with an unpaid servant at so slight an inconvenience to himself. The word "love" was never mentioned. Poor womankind, she is not far off the slave yet. A few years of childhood soon merges into slavery to the parents, exchanged for slavery to husband and mother-in-law, developing into slavery to children; from which she only wishes to gain her freedom, when taste for liberty is gone, to impress a new slavery upon a woman of the next generation. No wonder that when a woman revolts she does so more drastically than does man.

But poor Madame Sestrol's desire to find an English wife for her son only illustrates that persistent optimism of humanity which makes him believe that what he hasn't got is better than what he has, that optimism which in larger issues allows him to imagine that man will be less selfish, less self-seeking, less oppressive under new political regimes, which makes him dream of Utopia. . . .

How surprised she would be if she did get an English daughter-in-law! No English girl would do a half of the work Raymond's wife will have to undertake.

Raymond came late into his parents' life, he was a sickly and a tedious infant to rear, a delicate youth, and so, correspondingly beloved. For many years he lay with a rare illness of the kidney which caused a distortion of the glands of the neck. His mother took him to Lourdes without result, his father took him to a Parisian specialist, who cured the boy. Madame Sestrol is in a condition of divided belief in consequence: her reason tells her that Raymond was cured by drugs and human knowledge, her subconscience will not let go of the miracle for which she so devoutly hoped; she has formed a working compromise by which Lourdes prepared Raymond to receive the human aid. We have heard her say more than once that if it had not been for Lourdes Raymond would never have been cured at all.

The great affection which they bear for Raymond shows itself in a curious way—in exasperation. The peasant is terrified of one thing—of laziness. To him fainéant is the worst of epithets; where he might let off an assassin we feel sure that he would condemn a fainéant to death if he could. We are fainéant who hide our essential laziness beneath a show of painting pictures. Indeed, almost everyone is more or less fainéant who does not labour with hoe or with fork, anybody who is not bent under the Adamite curse in the most obvious way. For instance, we have heard the blacksmith dubbed fainéant. His smithy is annexed to a café run by his wife, and he is, we would imagine, a *warm* man. He is also a quick worker, taking indeed— for we rivalled it by chance one day—exactly the same time to fully reshoe a horse as I did to finish a small water-colour sketch. Much of his spare time he spends sitting in the shade of the market-place hangar gossiping with the consumptive baker. I don't know what he could do with more profit. He has a broad view of the competition between blacksmith and factory; he says, "The man who makes shoes or agricultural implements by hand is a fool, he can gain more profit by purchasing and reselling machine-made ones." So that when he is not employed in shoeing horses or cattle, when not engaged a-tiring wheels with a large bonfire on the main street, when not occupied in mending kitchen ranges, there is nothing for him to do. Yet he is almost a do-nothing, he doesn't work the earth.

Another " do-nothing " is the husband of the tobacconist-cooper's daughter. He is an ex-American soldier of French birth, pensioned with 700 francs a month—a fortune in the village—with severed nerves in the leg, dropped foot, and damaged pelvis. He has an ambition to become a violinist good enough to play in a cinema orchestra. The priests also are fainéant, and half the village rancour against the priests is due to the feeling that he earns his money without working for it.

Raymond is a lanky youth and his poor health in youth has not made a very robust man of him. He looks on the edge of Graves disease and his protuberant eyes have the startling effect of those of a pekingese or Chinese pug. Although he is a secretary to the Maire, for which he earns 2000 francs or roughly £26 a year, although in his spare time he fetches and carries for his mother, sometimes goes debt collecting in his father's place, and is continually walking over to his uncle's farm at Mazarolles, twelve kilometres there and back, to give a helping hand, he is perilously near being a fainéant.

The Sestrols cannot, of course, bear the idea that a son of their flesh should come near so dreadful a disgrace, and they are easily led to nag. His mother is especially hard upon him; but Raymond does not hesitate to answer back. He is quickly irritated. And so out of this deep-seated love burst out furious recriminations, like dog snappings, which luckily are short lasting. The doctor had ordered that Raymond must not be excited; still the peasant conscience cannot always be suppressed.

No wonder that they were terrified lest Raymond should bring home a fainéant wife. He had, unhappily, a taste for the showy rather than for the useful girl.

***

Raymond Sestrol, despite the almost animal snarlings and yappings which sometimes shrill through the kitchen door, is a good-humoured lad of the mildest of natures. He represents a curious element in French peasant life, since he was educated at a college in Albi, that town twenty-five miles to the south where amid weird heresies rose up a fortress cathedral, unique in ecclesiastical architecture, strange devotional monument to him who said, " He who takes the sword shall perish by the sword." Raymond is a queer fellow, a weakling, he lives in a world of strenuous imagination, in a fancy world of Balzacian supermen.

Conflict he shuns in practical life, he is, indeed, descendant of the valiant tailor who killed nine at a blow; but his imagination supplies all that his actual existence lacks. His stories all end in " Zim-boum "; Raymond's bump stories we called them. Whenever possible he was the author of the unholy crash which gives him such a raconteur's chance of a vigorous pantomime. He is the ideal audience for the American comic film. His favourite story was that of a village fête in which the band was mounted upon a two-wheeled cart which was propped at either end. Raymond noticed that the cart was leaning on one prop, and surreptitiously removed the other, with the result that a small movement amongst the players caused the cart to tip up, shot the band down the inclined plane and—Raymond's Zim-boum climax—flung the big drummer head first through his own instrument. Here are the skeletons of a few of his stories :

How the grave-digger, who is the local Gabriel Grubb, consorting too frequently with the wicker-covered bottle, went to finish an uncompleted grave, and how the burial party found him sound asleep at the bottom of it.

How the local Gabriel Grubb, after having drunk much freshly made Marc from the stills of the *bouilleurs de cru*, tried to get a drowned and bloated corpse into a coffin which was too small.

How the lightning fell in Janac just opposite to the Hôtel Sestrol, and how Madame Sestrol was nearly scared out of her wits because there was in the house for protection no candle blessed by the priest.

How a thunderbolt passed between a man's legs, on the

BLOCKED UP THE SPIGOTS OF THE FOUNTAIN.

road to Lafouille, killing two cattle upon the farther side of him.

How Raymond, one dusky evening, blocked up the spigots of the fountain and how the women, who each thought that another was stealing her water, came to blows.

How, having heard, in a *buvette*, the Maire say that he was about to call upon a certain old curmudgeon whom he feared to find abed at that hour, Raymond and some companions knocked up the curmudgeon beforehand, treating him to insults so that the Maire, coming in his turn, was welcomed with an unsavoury douche.

How a farmer, notorious for his litigations, hired three labourers whom he subsequently refused to pay, saying that they must sue him for the money; and how they dropped him down the well where they kept him till he paid.

How the collector of taxes and the courier came to blows about a barrel which had been stove in. (N.B.—This, happening while we were in Janac, we investigated to find that the blows existed wholly in Raymond's imagination.)

How a lad came up for his conscription medical examination, and how they made him drunk by putting the parings of finger nails into his wine, and how he behaved outrageously before the doctor. (Local tradition holds that finger-nail parings are most potent as intoxicants.)

Alas, many of Raymond's tales we lost! He talked fast and indistinctly; his language, in spite of his *education*, blurred by patois. The nearer he approached the climax, the faster, the more indistinct did he become, till he exploded with a whirl of arms, a fist on the table, Zim-boum in ejaculation and a hurricane of laughter. There was one about the *garde champetre* which he told us at least six times, but we never could make head or tail of it.

Raymond's principal business seemed to be the listing of Spaniards who came into Janac in dusky groups, odorous and unwashed, to work upon the railway. The Frenchman does not like these strangers whom lack of labour forces him to hire: they are counted as pariahs and as dangerous. It is curious how prejudiced we are against a dusky skin, associating it with a suppressed eagerness to kill. Personally I believe that the Spaniard is no more easily excited to a weapon than is the Southern Frenchman.

Till we noted the rich olive of these Spanish complexions we had scarcely marked how fair are the Janacquois, but history gives them a descent from the blond Cadurci, who were a warlike and obstinate people.

These Spanish labourers were very discontented. There were no lodging-houses for their quarters, and they were stowed away in one of the numerous empty houses of which Janac is only too full. Straw was their bed, and they lived as best they could. Yet though the villagers shunned and feared them they were everywhere treated with the greatest courtesy. We were often amazed by the patience and politeness of Madame Sestrol as she listened to their poor attempts to become intelligible. But she shared, nevertheless, the universal belief that if one speaks one's own language slowly, loudly and badly enough the foreigner must understand sooner or later.

It was interesting also to note the disturbed courtesy with which Madame Sestrol refused the numerous workmen from the railway who were seeking cheap lodgings. She had decided that it was a poorly paying business. The workman expects the lowest terms naturally, but our good hostess explained that what ran away with the profits was the midday lunch basket.

"You eat your dinner," she said. "*Eh bien*, there remains over scraps of bread, bits of cheese, all that goes to the ducks. You do not finish your wine, so what remains in the bottle is still good. But with these workmen all that goes into the basket is pure loss, if he doesn't eat it himself he throws it away or gives it to a comrade."

So the young workmen were refused, and turned away with reluctant steps from our promising *auberge*. They went off with a despairing stoop: the dearth of lodging in Janac being greater than in any other place which we have seen.

IV

THE *JUGE DE PAIX* AND THE COURT OF JANAC

IF this were a Tuesday (which it is not) we would have a 2–1 chance of being less solitary on our green garden seat, where laziness and no work has tempted us to remain chatting or somnolent since breakfast-time. A couple, at least, of small round tin tables would be set in the shade of the acacia trees, and peasants in sable dress— black boots, black trousers, black blouses, black hats, black beards, black eyes—would be seated drinking coffee from long glasses, or beer—enlivened by a dose of carbonic acid gas in Potato's bottling establishment over the road—or red wine which is brought in casks from vineyards lying twenty miles to the south. The country reckons little of those strange *apératifs* of the French town-dweller, those drinks of daring hue and astonishing taste which are used either to appetize or to minimize the results of appetizing; like the device of an impecunious young man who used to calm his tailor's clamours for settlement by ordering more clothes. At one of the tables of funereally clad peasants a jaundice-faced townsman, dressed in straw hat, tail coat and trousers of black and white check, would be talking earnestly and with authority. The peasants are litigants, the townsman a barrister. They would be waiting, we would be waiting, for the *juge de paix*. Janac is a *chef-lieu-de canton*, we have our fortnightly courts.

The *juge de paix* comes presently, round about half-past ten, walking with the jerky decision of a celebrity. He looks not unlike Monsieur Poincaré, but it is a Monsieur Poincare drawn by Tenniel for *Alice in Wonderland*, and the aggressive eyebrows of the French first minister are here pruned into gentleness. We all get up and follow him in a ragged procession to the corner of the triangular place and thence downhill a dozen buildings to the Mairie. The *juge de paix* is not quite the equivalent of our Justice of the Peace, he is more domestic : nor does he handle crime. Judge of the peace indeed he is not : he is a human olive branch ; his crest is a dove ; his very questions—curious, naïve legal questions, French equivalents for the famous " Who is Connie Gilchrist ? "—have a coo in them.

Maupassant has immortalized the *juge de paix* in *Le Cas de Madame Luneau* and *Tribunaux Rustiques*. To an English reader these rustic comedies of law may appear exaggerations, yet although Maupassant died thirty years ago, and although in these thirty years the world has made unbelievable advances, our *juge de paix* might well have taken lessons from those invented by the French novelist. The judge's opening in *Tribunaux Rustiques*, " *Madame Bascule, articulez vos griefs,*" would seem to us at first glance written for farce had our *juge de paix* not used the identical phrase often enough : so, too, the judge's exaggerated simplicity in *Laças de Madame Luneau.*

" HIPPOLYTE : *Je m'éclaircie, monsieur le juge. Or, qu'elle voulait un enfant et qu'elle me demandait ma participation. Je ne fis pas de difficultés, et elle me promit cent francs.* . . .

" LE JUGE DE PAIX : *Je ne vous comprends pas du tout. Vous dites qu'elle voulait un enfant ? Comment ? Quel genre d'enfant ? Un enfant pour l'adopter ?*

" HIPPOLYTE : *Non, monsieur le juge, un neuf.*

" LE JUGE DE PAIX : *Qu'entendez vous par cet mots :* ' *Un neuf ?* ' "

As a general rule the *juge de paix* does not hold that serious angle toward the law which we would consider correct in an English magistrate.* To some extent the judge seems to take both the law he is administering as well as the pleader as a kind of joke; he is like a humorous master settling a difference between a cook and a housemaid, neither of whom he is willing to lose. Contrasting with this humour, sometimes tart on the part of the judge, is the ceremony of the court in which these rough-handed litigants—some of whom can only speak in patois, losing themselves in long-winded explanations—are dubbed officially le Sieur Lachose or le Sieur Untel; the women have also their ceremonious appellation, Madame Veuve Angèle Jupon *née* Linge; and the judge sometimes uses these pretentious sounding titles to whip up his satire.

To add to the strange quality of these village courts of justice is the passionate eloquence of the barristers. These are two as a rule, brought at some expense from Francheville, one a stolid rustic sort of a man who does generally confine himself to a blunt exposition of his client's case; the other, the most admired, the tail-coated, rather jaundiced individual before mentioned. He has the gift for pathos—and bathos too. Eloquence in France is a serious affair. The oration of Sergeant Buzfuz for Mrs. Bardell pales before some of the jaundiced barrister's *copia verborum* dealing with the matter of a branch illegally cut from a tree or a gate left swinging open from malice: to hear him on the depredations of an errant goat was to be flooded with as much emotion as would have served many an actor for Mark Antony weeping over the body of Cæsar.

⁎

Talking of errant goats reminds me of another of Sestrol's

* In spite of memories of Justice Darling.

adventures, an adventure which nearly led him into the jurisdiction of the *juge de paix*.

Sestrol said, with that faint air of aggressive pride which marked almost all his reminiscences :

"I don't suppose that there is a man in the world other than myself who has been actually paid, *paid* for going to sleep on duty."

We suitably expressed astonishment and interest.

THE ANGER OF MONSIEUR TREE-FROG.

"I was eight years old or so at the time," went on Monsieur Sestrol, "and was night herdsboy in charge of a flock of goats. My master was a good sort of a man but quarrelsome, and embittered against his neighbour. Well, *mes amis*, one night I fell asleep while the goats wandered off into the lands of my master's enemy. In that night they cleared goodness knows how much of a vineyard. I awoke to find the goats gone. I hunted in the dawn, discovered them, drove them back unseen.

"My master goes out in the morning and hears that his enemy, in a towering rage, is coming to claim damages. He runs to me. 'Now, my lad,' he says, 'I don't care a rap where those goats were last night, but one thing I do know: understand that they were never out of your sight, and that they did *not* go into the lands of Monsieur "Tree-Frog"'—for so he nicknamed his neighbour.

"Monsieur 'Tree-Frog' comes raging in. My master meets him with a face of ignorance and astonishment: turns him on to question me. But no truth can Monsieur 'Tree-Frog' get. I lie and lie with so straight a face that he is dumbfounded. 'So much cunning and so young,' cried Monsieur 'Tree-Frog' at last and goes away baffled.

"For that my master gave me a whole five-franc piece, more than I had ever possessed at a time in my life till then, my wages being paid to my parents, you understand."

The Mairie is a large plain-fronted building of three stories covered with ochre wash which is mottled and peeling, on which the word "Mairie" is written in gilt letters. A large round door leads into the building and one of the windows is protected by a grille of wrought iron of curious workmanship. On the peeling walls are pasted notices, the one against flies, that proclaiming the subsidy of calves and pigs at the market, some prohibitions to shoot over certain farms, a demand for a tender to carry the mails to a distant village, one or two notices of property sales: just the every-day interests of the community.

The passage in the Mairie is dark and leads to the State school for girls, the innocent sounds of which occasionally can be heard through the court-room floor. Somewhere here, too, is stowed a fire-engine and the village big drum

which the cobbler has silenced. A broad flight of stairs leads to a landing on the first floor, from which opens out the Mairie's council chamber and the court-room.

The council chamber has a large green baize-covered table at which the councillors of the village seat themselves solemnly and do their simple best to retard progress. Here generally one can find Raymond asleep, his bulging forehead couched upon a pile of municipal literature, snoring away his 2000 francs per annum. The chamber of justice is small and whitewashed. A railing divides it into two, on the far side of which is the judge's table, also green covered, raised on a dais. To his left a lower table serves the clerk of the court by whose side a couple of chairs seat the barristers, who here plead without robes or bands. Nor does the judge himself mount signs of office, he sits rather plumply rubicund, half bored, half sardonic, with a large wen just appearing where his hair is thinning. There are chairs, half a dozen or so, at the disposal of an audience, but usually there is no audience. The litigants gather on the landing of the Mairie, and creep in bashfully as their names are called by the *greffier*.

"Le Sieur Anselm Chose contre Madame Paulette Machin," etc.

The litigants are of several varieties. There is the chronic plaintiff, usually a woman; there is the chronic defendant, usually a man. Both are egoists, the first too conscious of her neighbour's vices, the second too unconscious of his neighbour's rights. A type of the first was remarkable enough to be worthy of notice. She was an ex-nun who had left her convent to marry, but who has remained a devotional bigot. She was a lank, lean woman, with a pallid face ridged like plough land and two black pearls of eyes. She crossed herself whenever she passed the Hôtel Sestrol because Raymond had said in jest that he and his family were atheists ; but no Christian *charity* disturbed her conscience. She snapped into law at the slightest pretext, the terror of her neighbours.

Both types of litigants are well known to the *juge de paix*, who greets them with a rough grunt something like that of a hoarse pig :

" *Euh, euh ! Qu-est-ce que vous ronge cette fois-ci.*"

There is the litigant who talks as though there can be no question on the other side, and the litigant who hardly dares to state his own case ; there is the amicable litigant who can be seen drinking with his opponent before entering the Mairie and who has another drink with him to toast the decision whichever way it may be ; there is the sly litigant who tries clownishly to hide essential facts, but who is almost invariably brought to book with acid comments by monsieur le juge ; there is the hysterical witness ; the silent witness ; the loquacious. To all the judge is a sort of legal Father O'Flynn, sometimes forced to translate his decisions into patois when his suitors cannot understand the French. But often the litigants who do know French are unable to understand the legal form of the judge's summing up and stand silent, perplexed and gaping at the bar until the *greffier* chases them on to the landing ; where they still hang about wondering *how* things have *actually been* decided between them.

* * *

The more serious village affairs do not come before the *juge de paix*, they go to the tribunal at Francheville. Sometimes, however, the judge is an echo of the Francheville court, for instance, in a case of assault, the victim pleads for damages in the village after the aggressor has been punished officially in the town. Thus the aggressor pays double law expenses. A serious case occurred while we were in Janac : a *crime passionnel*, such as the French love.

It began in the old way: " There was a man and his wife and a *tertium quid* ; " but the story took a new turning. The triangle—shape of perfect stability, as the cynic called it—had persisted blatantly for many years until for some reason the woman repented or became tired of her lover. Bitter words were exchanged and the matter seemed to have died down. However, Janac awoke one morning to drama. The lover, an ex-Colonial soldier, having drunk too deeply on the night before, at about eleven o'clock had gone to the house of his ex-mistress to reassert his claim of rights. Something exasperated him and he gave the woman a box on the ears, in front of her husband and family. The latter set upon him, overwhelmed him by numbers, broke his head with the helve of an axe, dragged him to the stable and tied him by his legs to a ring high up in the wall, so that he half dangled, head downwards, " pouring his blood," as Raymond graphically described it, " into the *purée* of the cattle." Meanwhile the terrified neighbours had locked themselves in. The man was not released till the morning, and for some days was expected to die.

However, he did not die, and after a short period was walking about, his head elaborately plastered by Dr. Saggebou. Then the village prepared for further tragedy. " He is a Colonial," the gossips muttered one to another. " Everyone knows that the Colonial soldiers are bad men to fall across with. He is as tough as any. There will be murder done for this."

So we waited, waited for the tragedy.

One of the participants in the affair—a daughter—was pointed out to us by Raymond. She was a lame girl with the face of a Christmas supplement, a heavenly musician. Then the son, the helve-wielder, went by. Madame Sestrol indicated him with a respectful finger. He had surely not many days to live.

But the tragedy petered out. Summoned to the court at Francheville the terrible Colonial refused to bear witness against his assailants, some of whom were probably his own children; the village breathed once more in security.

Yet murder did come to us, both present murder as well as past crime. A girl of eighteen, turned out by her uncle, having given birth all alone hidden in a hayloft, strangled her illegitimate child. The baker was furious. He waved his thin fingers under the face of Potato who, being fat, was inclined to leniency. The baker, who had smashed a comrade's foot for a careless insult, was self-righteously indignant with this half-distraught baby killer.

"We must finish with these self-taken liberties," he coughed hoarsely. "No pity. Off with her head."

But she was acquitted. The French look with what appears to the English a lenient eye upon murder. Murder they seem to consider a crime only in dastardly cases. Give murder an epithet, tag it on to some perturbation of spirit, and the slayer escapes. Love, jealousy, hate, anger, fear, political passion, or even commercial interest, are held to be spiritual cyclones which acting on the normal humanity can whirl it outside of itself—beside himself, as we say—and so a crime committed outside of humanity is considered almost outside of the law. A curious feature of psychology this, that these French who are so primitively mosaic in their politics—an eye for an eye, a tooth for a tooth—should have travelled so far away from that boasted basis of human security, a life for a life. They do not hold that a misdeed committed in individual frenzy is to be balanced by another misdeed committed in communal revenge; they do not hold that for murder, the last unpardonable theft, restitution can be made by a forfeiture in kind. Still, *we* must think the French very lenient in murder. It was a question of café debate whether Landru, the modern Bluebeard, would not get off. A barrister, playing with his eloquence upon the heart-strings of a jury—which one must confess often seems to carry emotionalism beyond the limits of even a farce—has released how many assassins back into society. It is true that murder rarely becomes a habit. But we remember a satirical article in a French paper proving the only person one might not murder with impunity to be the total stranger, since no sentimental excuse could be found for murdering him.

So that the scene which we witnessed one afternoon, the return of a murderess—not the baby killer—to her village, cannot be so rare a spectacle in France as it would be in England. Before she reached us the rumour fled in front of her :

"She is coming, she is coming."

The village appeared unaltered. We sat quietly on our bench where we had been since luncheon. The exterior of the village still was deserted, but the windows, usually so many blank panes, were now spectacles, glasses through which Paul Prys, male or female or children, took stock with curious and almost respectful eyes of this fellow villager come "back to life." Was she really a strange-looking woman, or did our shocked senses lend her an air of strangeness —unwarned, would we have noticed her? Her face was like one of Modigliani's shorter-nosed models—sentimental eggs, a satirical critic dubbed them—but this woman had become startled and old, she seemed amazed to find the streets once more about her. Her face was a pallid mask in which those amazed eyes stared darkly, and from which the thin, grey, uncovered hair was drawn tightly back to a mere knob of a bun at about the Iceland of her skull. She went rigidly through the village with but brief glances to right or to left, supporting legs, rheumatic from prison, with the aid of two sticks. If she encountered a villager of bygone acquaintance she gave a dry little nod, "Eh! Joseph"— to which he would reply, "Eh! Suzanne"—and pass on.

We think that she appreciated and was enjoying the sensation she aroused.

No sooner was she gone beyond earshot than the curious sauntered into the street regarding her distant back.

"She killed her husband with a coal-hammer;" said Madame Sestrol to us. "It was a bad marriage. Always squabbling. Then one day she picked up the coal-hammer and just hit him. Here," and she indicated the temple.

We were on our road home when we met Madame St. Mouxa coming from her ex-aristocrat husband's shop.

THE MURDERESS.

There is nothing aristocratic about Madame St. Mouxa: her husband might decorate up well enough into a Seigneur, but she, though she gives herself a hundred beauty airs, remains unalterably the over-plump little bourgeoise that she is. Madame St. Mouxa is the incarnation of the obvious.

If one shows her a bottle she will say with a pretty air of wisdom, "That is a bottle, you put liquid into it and stop it with a cork"; and if you are looking at a dog she will say, "That is a dog, it is of a yellow colour, has four legs, one at each corner, runs about and barks." Rather like Mr. Hilaire Belloc's strategy for beginners during the war. Poor Madame St. Mouxa, she is vain, and doubtless when she was seventeen had a certain enticing roundness which she mistook for beauty. Rotundity has now gone out of fashion even in provincial France, but Madame St. Mouxa has become rounder. Her little son let out to us a fact which doubtless Madame St. Mouxa would rather have kept a close secret.

"Mother thinks she is getting fat, she is taking castor-oil regularly to become thinner."

Il faut souffrir pour être belle, but Madame St. Mouxa does not know that castor-oil, in spite of its obvious effects, is a fattening medicine.

She now met us, and said with the painstaking precision of a governess:

"That woman is a murderess, she has committed murder. She chopped open her husband's head with an axe, yes. She hit him once and then came back to hit him again, that makes twice, you understand. He walked up here after it had all happened. I saw him. His head was laid quite open and his brains were running down his face. That is a fact; by brains I mean the inside of his head, you know. And she was only put in prison during five years for so horrible a crime. Crime, you know, a misdeed, what! Five years, in prison, you understand, only that."

In the evening we drew a few more facts from Madame Sestrol.

"Chopper? Nonsense!" she said. "Hit him with the

coal-hammer, a *little* coal-hammer it was, lying on the table, just there, as you may say, and she picked it up in a temper and gave him a back-handed stroke, without looking, just as she was running from the room—didn't know that she *had* hit him till she got back. Then it might have been all right, only they left it for four days—till it all went bad inside his head. 'Brains running down?' Nonsense! Who has been telling you all that stuff? Geneviève St. Mouxa doesn't know anything about it. Why they came here on their way to Dr. Saggebou. She was supporting him, holding him up and crying upon his shoulder. 'Have I done thee any injury, my cabbage? have I harmed thee? who would never hurt a hair of thy head.'

"And the doctor called them fools; but there was no getting over the fact that all the inside of his head had gone bad. They said that he must have been a strong man to have walked up here and down again in that state. But those two were never well suited, aways squabbling till the neighbours *said* there'd be murder done one day. In fact, once before she did try to poison him with wash for the vines, but he got over it. Not a good home for the children, no. So the saintly sisters took them, but now doubtless the mother will want them back again. They would be better where they are now, because, after all, the woman isn't quite——" she tapped her forehead; "nor was the man either, to my thinking," she added.

The *juge de paix* does not touch such grave matters as these. He travels about from canton to canton, an affable, slightly pompous, slightly sardonic, peace-maker, an ambulating olive branch dipped in vinegar.

* * *

Here is a typical morning's work for the *juge de paix*. He begins with a few cases of police work, riding bicycles without lamps, etc. These are polished off rapidly, in some cases only a fine of a franc is imposed, but expenses bring it up to fifteen or twenty francs, so the culprit doesn't get off as easily as it appears on the surface. Then the village *placier* brings in a man who refused to pay rent for the pavement he occupies. The French merchant, it is well  known, spreads part of his shop outside upon the street. The commune has decided that all merchants shall pay for this privilege, fifty centimes per metre per day, or a commutation for a year—Sestrol pays thirty francs per annum for some six metres. But an old hard-shelled-looking villager objects; he has used his pavement for so many years without cost, new-fangled ideas rouse his gall. The judge rules that a commune can make its own laws, the old conservative is waved away still protesting.

"Le Sieur Bossot contre le Sieur Gaudat," cries the *greffier*. Two black-clad peasants slouch into the room, they stand stockily in their black blouses, fumbling their black felt hats on the railing.

"*Exposez vos griefs*," says monsieur le juge.

The *greffier* gabbles from a paper that le Sieur Bossot objects to a duckpond constructed by le Sieur Gaudet which is unhealthy and a nuisance, the said duckpond being constructed by blocking up the public gutter between the houses of the said Sieurs Bossot and Gaudet. (Madame Sestrol does the same over against the grille just beyond Potato's.)

Monsieur Bossot speaks in an injured voice; "*Ça pue*," he repeats with growing emphasis: Monsieur Gaudet contradicts him and is told to wait his turn. Monsieur Gaudet, his turn come, claims custom, "My grandfather before me." The judge says custom cannot cover insanitary nuisances and refers the case to an arbiter; let them choose somebody from their own hamlet, somebody with position; he suggests a few names. Les Sieurs Bossot and Gaudet are not satisfied; those of whom Bossot approves are repudiated by Gaudet, and *vice versâ*.

"Well, it will cost you more," says the judge. "I am here to save you money if I can, but if you won't have it, *tant pis*." And he appoints a surveyor from Francheville.

Most local questions of this nature, such as rights of way, locking of gates, damage by beasts, illegal trimming of another man's hedge, and so on, are *always* referred to local arbitration. The peasants know this, yet such is their love of legal squabble that they persist in going to the expense of coming before the *juge de paix* for such matters.

The next claimant is of the cunning type. He wants to have an order that his opponent must move his strawstack to another part of the local common-land. It now blocks a gate of the claimant's; opponent has refused to move, so claimant has been forced to law. But the defendant proves that the position of his stack counts back for several generations, that the gate was only newly made last winter.

This moves the judge to pig-like noises.

"Euh, Euh!" he cries, wagging a finger at the claimant. "You want to trick me into upsetting old customs, do you? You know perfectly well that I'll do no such thing."

Then comes one of the habitual belligerents whom the judge greets with:

"Hallo, you here again! What do you want this time?"

The prosecutrix is a tall woman, built exactly like a wooden grenadier in a skirt; her clothes are black and rusty; her bonnet sticks up from her head like a busby made of wire, weatherbeaten silk chiffon and jet ornaments.

She voices her complaints against two cousins, a lean, dark, eagle-nosed man and a peaky, anxious-looking woman

THE VILLAGE COURT.

with large, pendulous red hands. It appears that they have been cutting branches from trees on her land.

"Eh bien?" asks the judge, cocking his head at the couple.

The man gesticulates his defence, his wife stands on tiptoe with anxiety. They have a right of way for animal traffic, the pugnacious old woman—always at loggerheads with her neighbours and with her relations more acidly than with any —has planted trees so that now they have grown up they spread across this right of way. The man has merely cleared a passage for a laden donkey with panniers, his right. This planting of the trees is recent, malicious.

"Arbitration," says the judge; then to the married couple, "You have a right to passage, of course."

"I won't accept it," snaps the old grenadier; "I'll take it to a higher court."

Out thrusts the judge's chin.

"Euh, Euh!" he grunts. "You think you know better than I do, eh? You know so much law that you're a regular *avoué*, yes?"

The old grenadier puts on a face of mulish obstinacy, her body goes tense with antagonism.

"I'll go to a higher court," she repeats viciously, in a creaking voice.

"All right," shouts the judge, flinging himself back into his chair. "Waste your money if you want to. I'm not here to nurse fools. But you'll lose, I tell you that beforehand."

The next case comes into court arguing, a tall woman and a short one; the short one carries an earthen pot in her hand which she shakes under her opponent's nose.

"Silence!" calls the *greffier*, and reads out the document of the case:

"Madame Veuve Paturel claims against Madame Veuve Sorbet the value of a pot of goose grease delivered by the latter to the former in a condition unfit for use."

"Madame Paturel?" says the judge.

"Monsieur le juge," replies the woman with the pot.

"Prénom?"

"Angeline," replies the woman, brandishing the pot.

"Name before marriage?"

"Belot."

"Madame Veuve Angeline Paturel née Belot, articulez vos griefs," says the *juge de paix*.

Madame Paturel has sold her property to Madame Sorbet. She has sold it under an annuity agreement—common enough in the district, where hard cash counts for so much—that Madame Sorbet shall provide her during her lifetime with the necessities of life in kind, so many pots of goose grease for the kitchen, so much firewood for the winter, so much provender for a horse, so many sacks of wheat for bread, etc.—a kind of agreement productive of much bickering. One pot of goose grease delivered has proved to be bad. She has reclaimed it without result.

Madame Paturel glares vindictively at Madame Sorbet and waves her *pièce de conviction*.

Madame Sorbet, undisturbed by the demonstration, answers, with calmly folded arms and a prim expression, that the pot was good *when* it was given to Madame Paturel.

"Oho, and when was it given?" asks the judge, turning to Madame Veuve Paturel.

She begins to talk volubly, incoherently.

"Last January," says Madame Sorbet with cold triumph.

"And did you examine it at the time?" asks the judge.

"Bad grease is bad grease, monsieur le juge," snaps Madame Paturel. "Nothing will alter that."

"But good grease can turn into bad grease," retorts the judge. "Did you examine it?"

"But smell it, monsieur le juge," cries Madame Paturel, leaning as far as she can over the barrier, endeavouring to thrust the offending pot beneath the judge's nose. "*Puez le, mais puez le seulement.*"

"I'm not here to smell pots of grease," shouts the judge,

banging the table. "Answer me. When did you open this pot?"

"Ten days ago," mutters Madame Paturel. "But smell it only, monsieur le juge, smell it only, I pray you."

She turns furiously on Madame Sorbet, who, at last losing her enforced calm, retorts with energy. The two women quarrel loudly in the court-room. At last they are urged outside the door, where they stay quarrelling on the landing. The next case cannot be begun. At last, still vociferating, they are thrust downstairs, out into the street, their voices die away into the distance.

The two final cases are referred back to their hamlets for arbitration: one that of a gate illegally locked across a right of way; the second a case of cutting back the branches of a wild cherry tree which, standing in the plaintiff's ground and therefore his property, was overshadowing a part of the defendant's garden.

A hush follows the last case.

"The next," says the judge.

"That is all," replies the *greffier*.

"Euh!" answers the *juge de paix*, and stretches his arms.

We, his only audience, get up from our corner—where we quietly seat ourselves each fortnight—give him a non-committal bow, and steal softly on our string-soled shoes down the stairs, out into the streets, to the Hôtel Sestrol, where some of the adversaries are now toasting each other in *pinard*, the red wine of the country; or are already enjoying a midday meal of Madame Sestrol's cooking.

* * *

Our prize case roused the whole village to malicious laughter. Madame Veuve Giard summoned Monsieur

Rothou for defamation of character. She deposed that le Sieur Rothou had called her a "*pute*" and that he had further said that Mademoiselle Giard—her daughter—was "*se trainant dans le bazar*" at Toulouse. Madame Veuve Giard, an habitual litigant, was prognathic in two ways— she had an underhung jaw and an underhung stomach— she was very short and the whole of her small being was

TOASTING EACH OTHER IN PINARD.

consumed with bitterness against le Sieur Rothou, from whom she was claiming 2000 francs damages. (In strict law this case could not come before the *juge de paix*, who is limited to cases up to 1000 francs.)

Monsieur Rothou, a pasty-faced, unpleasant-looking young man, who appeared quite capable of having said all that Madame Giard claimed, and more, was riposting with a counterclaim. Madame Giard, he said, had begun the quarrel, she had called him "*Cain*," he only asked for 3000 francs compensation.

There were witnesses, and the process, opened late one Tuesday, was set back for a fortnight.

The witnesses of Madame Giard, four in number, were incoherent and probably truthful. They testified to the mutual nature of the recriminations, to the respective positions of the quarrellers, but more precise details were not to be had from them. Madame Giard's last witness, a young postman—lacking one hand from the war, a man whose round averaged twenty miles a day—said that the two parties were using bad language mutually.

"What kind of language?" cried the judge. "Be precise."

"Oh," said the postman, "*un peu de tout, quoi.*"

"Be more exact," insisted the judge.

"Oh, well——" said the postman, getting embarrassed.

"*Pute*, for example?" prompted the judge.

"Well, yes, perhaps," said the postman reluctantly.

"And *Cain.*"

"A bit of all sorts," insisted the postman. "Just the sort of words that you or I would use if we lost our tempers, you know."

"I don't know at all," replied the judge grumpily, and set him free.

As each witness stepped down the judge read out his evidence, queried if it were correct, told the witness to sign his statement and asked if he wished to claim for expenses. None of the witnesses for Madame Giard claimed expenses. They all felt that they had done too little for their appellant; in fact, they were conscious that they had almost betrayed her.

Monsieur Rothou had also four witnesses. We do not

think that a clearer case of concerted perjury was ever exhibited in a court. It was evident that all had sat down at a table and had learned off their statement.

"On the fifth of July at about half-past six I was standing in the street near the castle. Madame Veuve Giard was at her door, Monsieur Rothou was at his garden gate. Madame Giard without provocation addressed him in jeering tones, later calling him '*Cain*' and '*bâtard*.'"

"Did he call her '*pute*'?" asked the judge.

"We did not hear it," replied witness.

"Nor the other thing, what was it?" said the judge, referring to the paper. "Oh yes, about her daughter '*se trainant dans le bazar à Toulouse*.'"

"Not to our knowledge," answered each witness, who each eagerly claimed expenses.

The judge summed up thus:

"In view of the fact that Madame Veuve Clémence Giard, *neé* Proprecote, has accused le Sieur Celestin Magloire Rothou of defamation, of calling her a '*pute*' and further stating that her daughter is walking the streets in Toulouse; in view of the fact that le Sieur Rothou has counterclaimed against the Veuve Giard that she called him '*Cain*' with intent of injurious meaning, in view further of the fact that we do not find that the Veuve Giard has proved her accusation whilst the Sieur Rothou has substantial evidence for his statement, we condemn the widow Giard to pay to the Sieur Rothou twenty-five francs damages and the whole cost of the case."

He looked over at Madame Giard, who stood angry and baffled, resenting the judge's acceptance of what seemed to be an obvious perjury; he looked at her and thrust his white imperial forward at her as if to say, "That will teach you to bring frivolous cases to me."

The verdict caused general pleasure in the village. Monsieur Rothou was no favourite, but Madame Giard was detested. During the past winter she had killed three valuable sporting dogs of her neighbour's by leaving poisoned eggs for them to eat. The chemist was implicated in that affair. Madame Giard had got over his good nature with a false story; still, he was imprudent in giving to the woman the poisoned eggs. They said that it cost him a pretty penny to hush the matter up.

V

PEASANTS AND VILLAGERS—LIFE AND CUSTOMS

WE should be lucky if we got out of court before 11.30, by which time the litigants are dining, burying satisfaction or disappointment under spoonfuls of *soupe* and sopped bread-crusts. Three occasions bring the countryman into Janac: court days, market days, and Sundays. On market days he lunches, and on court days also; on Sundays he generally goes home for the weekly dinner after Mass. In this part of France the peasantry lunches early, as early as eleven o'clock on most of the farms, and by 11.30 the Hôtel Sestrol is already filled with black-clad figures almost invisible in the dark interior, but audible at their *soupe*.

We think it may be said that of all the peasantry of Europe the Frenchman alone has a proper appreciation of gastronomy. Our friend, the gastronomer, Fritz Vanderpyl, has written: "The German feeds himself; the Englishman, according to his social status, repairs the wastes of the day; the Italian eats with an eye to economy; only the Frenchman dines, recognizing under all circumstances the value of the viands he is tasting." Seeing the delicacy and care with which Madame Sestrol provides for her peasant guests we are bound to agree on the lower levels, though we will not venture to do justice between epicureans. An English farmer takes his slice of beef with roughly done potatoes and cabbage and plenty of mustard, the German is content with a dish of *Sauerkraut* and boiled sausages, but the French peasant has his *soupe*, his boiled beef and salted cucumber, his fried chicken, his salad, his cheese and his coffee " watered " with a dash of cognac. He is served liberally, but helps himself with taste; eating carefully but not immoderately. There is, in this district, one curious habit. Having finished his *soupe* the peasant pours into his plate a sup of wine which he drinks from the edge of the dish, lifting it to his lips. We wonder from whence arose this curious custom ?

* *
*

It is difficult, perhaps, not to be led into those facile generalizations which come to a foreigner so easily. It is so effective to sum up the image of " Frenchman " with a few terse phrases. Yet, truthfully speaking, does such a thing as a type of *Frenchman* exist ?

Your dweller in the country-side, for instance, despises the Frenchman of Paris * : to him the Parigot is an alien, almost a foreigner. Only that Parisian is welcomed who was once a native of the village, and even he, on his periodical returns, is surrounded with some of the atmosphere which attaches to the repatriated Frenchman Lemoule (now an American citizen, having fought in her armies). Nor, in turn, does the provincial absorb himself into Paris as an Englishman merges himself into London. It takes as many generations to make a Parisian as to make an American, and the provincials who crowd to the capital hold somewhat aloof, settling in localities usually situated near to the termini at which they arrive ; only the Auvergnat one finds disseminated ; and, as the Parisian remarks, " wherever you find an Auvergnat you'll probably find a bed-bug."

* " Le peuple de Paris est si sot, si badaud, si inept par nature."—RABELAIS.

The type we conventionally depict for the Frenchman—dark, small, excitable, exaggerated, over-dressy and gesticulating—is the very type at which the larger part of the dwellers in France laugh. He is the Toulousain or the Marseillais, he may have come to England in considerable numbers connected with the wine trade, and so assumed a national type. Here in the Rouergue the peasants are easy mannered, merging towards the stolidity of the inhabitants of Auvergne, which lies east of us. One is going to be easily tempted to gene-  ralization, and one is tempted for a definite reason. When all is said and done the future civilization rests on the shoulders of the peasant. He is your final chairman who has the casting vote. The Russian Utopia, all our funny little Utopias, break on the back of the land worker. Commerce, industry, etc., are only the bees which suck the honey from the flowers rooted in the soil; if the plants refuse to bear flowers, the bees die. So that " back to the land " is a slogan full of fine purpose though as impracticable as any other idealism.

It has been the habit of a certain set of Utopians to hold up the French system of peasant proprietorship as the sole method of preserving national prosperity. We were to make England a land " fit for heroes " by giving retired soldiers plots of arable land and by pushing them out into the

94 PEASANTS AND VILLAGERS—

dreariness of the country. The delights of tilling for one's self were presumed to overbalance all other more convivial enjoyments. But, to inquire more closely into how the recent developments of French peasant proprietorship work, let us look a little more closely at Janac. Here we have a village of peasant proprietors: within the memory of living persons it has lost at least one-third of its inhabitants.

Under the *peasant* system, peasant proprietorship gives an exaggerated amount of work for little result. Let us take, as an example, the cooper-tobacconist—father-in-law to Monsieur Lemoule, ex-American soldier. The cooper owns his house in the village where he lodges his mother, his daughter and her husband. The daughter makes hats and *lingerie* and sells a few tapes and ribbons, the mother looks after the tobacco shop, the cooper with the inadequate help of Lemoule, who is a war relic, tends his fields and pursues his trade. The fields themselves are scattered: two miles to the east, on the top of a hill, is a small vineyard; a mile and a half to the south is another; a mile and a half to the east-nor'-east is a hayfield; a mile and a half to the north-east is a field under corn, half a mile farther on in the same direction is a field of cabbages; along the railway line to the west, some three miles away, in a deep valley very difficult to get at, is a patch of brushwood for winter fires, coal being dear in Janac; and about a mile away, on the point of a hill, separated from Janac by a deep valley and the river so that the road makes nearly four miles of loops to travel there, is a wood of chestnut trees, from which he gathers chestnuts and cuts his material for barrel staves. The haphazard chances of land division, of marriage or inheritance have brought all these detached pieces of land into his possession. To predict a little further, he may be expected to leave these intact to his daughter. To the west, deep in the valley, Lemoule has a childless uncle with other scattered property, so that probably Lemoule may inherit yet another patch or two to add to *his* sons' dispersed occupation. It must be clear to an ordinary intelligence that farming under these conditions can be neither productive of enthusiasm nor of profit.

A natural result of this scattering of property is that the village home becomes the farmhouse. From all these outlying unguarded fields the crops must be carted into the homestead which cannot afford the elbow room of a farm. So the livestock go into the basement with the wine vats—the *basse-cour*—from which the effluvia of pigs, chickens, ducks, rabbits and oxen filter up through every cranny till, as we have already said, the inhabitants are steeped in the odour of their cattle. The produce goes into the loft, hay, corn, brushwood, cabbages, potatoes, maize, etc., where it remains a danger in case of fire, and no small breeder of fleas.

Here the intelligent Utopian begins to protest: "Yes, but why don't—— ?" Unfortunately, as soon as one has recourse to "Why don't ?" in dealing with humanity one is lost. There are a million obvious "why don'ts ?" which nobody has ever yet solved. Utopia is only just round the corner, and "why don't ?" is the signpost; but no one ever turns that way. The peasants don't concentrate on their farms first because they are peasants: for exactly the same pigheaded prejudices which bring them futilely squabbling into the court of the *juge de paix* on Tuesdays. Besides, suppose a peasant has land which affords him a bare subsistence, how is he to afford—even if he wanted to— the arbitration fees which would attend the most simple piece of land exchange ? Moreover, corn land, hay land, chestnut land, brushwood and vineyard do not lie near one another in these hills.

No! the small proprietor, complicated by family division and succession, does not seem a really satisfactory solution to all agrarian difficulties. The result is—depopulation.

Inevitably the old abuse of landlord and tenant will spring up once more, and the vicious circle is begun again.

But a curious result of this peasant proprietorship is

VEGETABLES.

annoying to the would-be visitor—I do not mean to a restaurant visitor such as ourselves, but to one who would take rooms and begin housekeeping at home. In Janac there is a butcher (who sells rarely aught but veal), a baker and many grocers, but not one root of vegetable, not one basket of fruit, not one head of cabbage or salad can the intruder purchase. Each peasant proprietor plants only enough for his own family; if he sells he will be forced to buy later on for his own supply. This year was exceptionally dry, a drought to be precise. Janac starved for vegetables, but the only green stuff which reached the village was that brought by a market gardener and his wife who came speculatively on a Sunday from a distance of sixteen kilometres.

A proverb in patois is apt on this matter:

> " Quan lou rixe biro la gabello
> Lou paoure emplino l'escudelo."

" When the rich must turn his hay, the poor will fill his vegetable basket."

But this year the hay was spread and dried to the rich man's whole satisfaction.

* * *

Indubitably the only able-bodied man who stays here buried in the country without a private income or a Government job is the man who cannot get away. One and all the dwellers in Janac bemoaned their lot.

" Eh, it's all very well for you, coming here in the summer," they protested, " but try the winter. Then you'll see."

The consequence is that Janac, peasant-owned though it be, will be more and more setting its face to the town. The eldest son must remain to till the soil, the others can develop. The French peasant differs from his compeers in some other lands in that he has no prejudice against book-learning. He may say " fainéant," but he is not averse to his children mounting in the social scale. And mount they do in an extraordinary fashion. Let us take our little *place*, the triangle before the Hôtel Sestrol. Here are the shops of the baker and of the *épicier*-cobbler (not St. Mouxa, we remind you). The *épicier*-cobbler is a small old man, bowed with rheumatism. He pursued a diversity of trades, including the selling of sweets which are liable to be tinged with bits of cobbler's wax, as he scrapes them from their bottle with uncleaned fingers. His wife is tiny and has the face of a mask flattened by packing. The son of this peasant pair is an assistant in a large Paris shop, his wife is an elegant, good-humoured young *Parisienne*—though of Janaquois descent—who startles the village with the modernity of her overalls, when she comes to pay the annual ten days' visit to her husband's parents. Here we may note that the clannishness of the villager is such that often a man living in Paris will choose his wife from some family of other Parisianized compatriots, as in this instance. The husband is a healthy looking, intelligent townsman interested mildly in archæology, as a hobby, and he has a map of the castle as it was in the fourteenth and fifteenth centuries. The son of this family—still a child—is pure city bred. He has the alertness and the elegance of the city; his active mind, his daring, his very build is extraordinary when contrasted—as it is sharply here—with the awkward and bashful clumsiness of his village contemporaries. They strive to imitate him, and it is as if a carthorse would emulate a racer. Albert will become a professional man, a soldier, a doctor, a lawyer, probably. When the old people die the son will let both house and fields; he may sell them; certainly he will not return to Janac. Back to the country he may probably go in the end, but it will be to buy a shoddy villa in some *banlieu* of Paris, where he will drag out his declining years in the company of similar fugitive Parigots, finding sufficient country romance in a few ranks of cabbages and an arbour of clambering roses.

Compulsory military service must also have an influence on the depopulation of villages. Soldiering in barracks is doubtless hard enough, but it brings the youngster into close contact with the vulgar and virile delights of the town; a passion for green drinks can so easily drown a passion for green fields.

However, the French transitions upwards in society are not fraught with the tragedies of similar ascents in our country. There lives here an old good-for-nothing who has for years simulated decrepitude in order to exist on the labours of his wife, a poor village woman-of-all-work, hobbling painfully about her daily toils, one leg being longer than the other. The daughter went into service in Toulouse where she became the mistress of, and later wife to, a man of moderate means. Their two children are growing up, the son is soon entering an officer's training college, the daughter is well versed in all the frivolities of flapper vanity. Yet the family comes every year to spend a month during the summer in the company of the almost pauper parents.

Or again; the sempstress of the village has a tiny shop with two meagre rooms above it. She was agog with excitement. Her son, with his wife and baby, was coming to visit her. The son duly arrived in his car. It was too magnificent and too long to go into Sestrol's stable and garage-room was begged of Dr. Guibert in the faubourg. The wife was more elegant than the mother of Albert; obviously a young woman of excellent education. They remained ten days. The son is an engineer, his present state the result of a romance, as they count romance in France. It happened that the young woman, having looked over her male acquaintances, could see nobody who pleased her imagination as a husband; so having the conviction that the moment had come to marry, she put an advertisement in the paper couched thus:

"Young woman, twenty-one years of age, well-educated, dowry 100,000 francs, would like to meet a young man—profession engineer preferred—with a view to marriage."

Having read the advertisement young Vulcan went, saw and was conquered. His brother-in-law has installed him as manager of a factory of electrical fittings. The couple spent the *dot* on the long motor-car; and here they are, summering in the sempstress's two cramped rooms.

So that one day the sempstress's house will be vacant.

It is inevitable that the village will dwindle. Civilization being what it is, the day must come when large corporations will take over these chessboard farms and vineyards, welding them into commercial affairs under the heel of machines. Already the process has begun farther to the south. In the vineyards of the Midi, Gilbey, Potin, Nicholas and a crowd of other mercantile vine merchants are grasping the vineyards, turning the joyous cult of the grape into a factory business.

With reference to the marriage made by advertisement (not an uncommon procedure) we must at once admit that the French view marriage at an angle very different from our own. We English lay a sentimental stress upon this mysterious factor "love," irresistible mutual attraction, the positive and negative electrical, as it were; we suggest to our maidens that they should hold themselves aloof till this strange force approaches. Yet it would be rash to assert that this mysterious juxtaposer, Cupid, does his work with infallibility. How often may not the passion be aroused by a suitable conjunction of health, season, compatible male and suggestibility. Is it not Stendhal who says that not one person in a hundred would fall in love if he or she had not read about it? Jane Austen, whose values of humanity are extraordinarily sagacious, treats love as a much milder passion than we value it to-day: as indeed do most older writers.

So we skirmish round awaiting the great mutual attraction, love; we make tentative experiments called flirtation, in which only one side may be in earnest, until such an experiment discovers both sides to be mutually eager, from which marriage ensues as a rule. The French follow a different course, the young girl keeps herself prepared to fall in love as soon as a suitable man is provided; she is in love with her husband before he exists and has only to transfer the already existing emotion to the solid object (often a very solid object) presented to her. Yet even in France things are not quite impersonal. The young lady who put her advertisement so frankly in the paper had already canvassed the young men of her neighbourhood, she probably had weighed the advantages of a score of applicants drawn by the advertisement. No one seeing her with her husband could doubt for a moment the genuine love and happiness which she has reaped from marriage.

While we were in Janac the *fiançailles* of Mlle. Cécile Porphy were announced. She was a rich cousin of the wife of Lemoule and we had been invited to the house of her parents in order that Jo might play on the piano; for Mlle. Cécile had the village distinction of being a pianist. Her instructors had been nuns, first one of Janac itself, then a superior mistress, nun of Francheville. Cécile was an ambitious pianist, ill contented to remain within her powers.

She was especially the performer of a piece called "The Tempest" which moved the village to great admiration. At Jo's playing the people were amazed, but with that kind of amazement which comes from a juggling trick or legerdemain. To see fingers move thus rapidly was so enthralling that they forgot to listen to the music. But ah! when Mlle. Cécile played "The Tempest" ... that was another affair—that was Art. The thunder rumbled in the bass, the lightning jagged down the piano in discords, the wind howled in fumbled arpeggios up the treble, while the rain poured in a persistent rattle of B♭. The fact that the piece was a third beyond Mlle. Cécile's technique, that she had, it must be confessed, very little sense of rhythm, and that the piano was abominably out of tune, detracted little from the general effect; would it not be pedantry to expect storms to be in rhythm, and did not a few strange dissonances greatly add to the wildness of the interpretation?

Up till the moment of her engagement Mlle. Cécile was an ordinary, pretty girl who dressed with a little more taste than the average in the village: she also had a certain charm of gaiety. From the moment of her engagement she bloomed with that curious underglow, in itself a beauty, which the birth of love causes to pulsate, like a corona, about the one who loves. She became, almost at once, what would be called *genuinely* in love. The young man was nothing romantic to look at, rather too fleshy for his years, tending to a jolly pomposity—but quite unromantic. However, as Mlle. Cécile confided to Jo, " such a good position, you know, madame." That's the difference. We encourage love for the individual, the French lean towards love for the *State* of Matrimony, and in this state the position counts quite as much as the individual, indeed, more perhaps. How many a marriage which turns out a failure in poverty might not have been successful in riches.

Indeed, it may be argued that the *mariage de convenance* has greater chances of happiness than the marriage of love. Being in love rather with the condition than with the individual, the French bride has not to face the ordeal of discovering that her idol is too human after all—and almost every French girl can cook. It offends our sense of romance, that is true, but the point is that it does not offend against the French girl's sense of romance. After all, we are more creatures formed by habit than man in his vanity will admit; but every separate nation, every separate province, every separate household even, is convinced that *its* particular set of habits are the last and highest development possible to humanity.

However, is one not too often tempted to consider marriage in the light of its personal success between husband and wife ? From the community's point of view things look different; if the marriage is viewed from the angle of the children, the disaster of the French method becomes more apparent.*

* * *

For instance, this evil comes out in its worst light in the marriage of the *garde champêtre*. He is a man now of about fifty-five, robust, virile still, with a harsh grizzled

---

* We are, perhaps, taking it a little for granted that in England persons never marry for money reasons.

beard and hair which might be considered long for an Englishman. He is charged with the general municipal police matters of the community, cleanliness of streets, crying of communal decrees, chief fireman, inspector of nuisances and so on. He is a rude-tempered but not a harsh man, and he carries on the additional trade of saddler. As an example of how he performs his duty, came a scare of rabies in the district and the muzzling order was issued. The office of the *garde champêtre* was to see the order carried out. The muzzles were of a most curious variety. Kissme, the dog of the Hôtel Sestrol, soon divested itself of the hindering piece of leather about its face and went from thence on with the muzzle sticking out behind its ears, until the dog, tired of the nuisance, chewed off the projecting parts. Cora, the puppy from opposite, was put into a muzzle large enough for a mastiff, so that it could get its whole face through one of the openings; Oursa, the tobacconist-cooper's black dog, had a strap wound round its mouth so that either the poor dog could not open its mouth at all—and was tortured with thirst during the heat—or, when the strap had worked far enough down, could bite as easily as before the order was promulgated. In nine cases out of ten the muzzles were useless, and in five cases out of ten the dog divested its jaws of the muzzle which it carried dangling on the neck. As often as not the dog of the *garde champêtre* itself went unmuzzled. Not effectiveness seemed to be demanded, but merely some evidence of good will, a general acquiescence.

Wedded to this robust citizen was a withered, bent, quarrelsome, filthy old hag who could well have been posed as a witch out of *Macbeth*. She appears to be half idiot, daughter of that decrepit senile whom we have depicted on page 17, that old tottering crone whose many mad greeds have dwindled into one lingering desire for coffee. But the *garde champêtre* is rather proud of his marriage. He married well. He, a landless, portionless tradesman, has wedded an heiress. She owns two houses, a garden, vineyards, cornlands and brushwood. Rashly he had said, " She's dirty, yes, but I'll clean her up after marriage." He has not succeeded in his boast.

And it was the *garde champêtre* who sang us the song of " Lo Biéllo," which was perhaps cynical in a man of his achievements. We had supped out of doors at L'Escaret, the farm which Sestrol had bought. It was dusk, and supper over we were all reclining on the grass, Monsieur and Madame Sestrol, Raymond, Élise their girl lodger, the village sempstress, Raymond's uncle from Escarolles and the *garde champêtre*—he had left his wife at home. It was the feast day of the Railway Station. They were going to illuminate the castle with red flares; this old farm in the valley was an admirable point of view. To enliven the tedium of our waiting the *garde champêtre* was enticed to sing an old song in patois :

LO BIÉLLO.

Ce' d'ijn Paris ya uno Biéllo
Ce' d'ijn Paris ya uno Biéllo
Qu' axé aou mey quatrevint ans
Trin-tran-laboureuse
Qu' axé aou mey quatrevint ans
Trin-tran-laboureusement.

Lou dimenxe à lo gleio
Lou dimenxe à lo gleio
Cen pas assieta pret d'un galant
Trin-tran-laboureuse
Cen pas assieta pret d'un galant
Trin-tran-laboureusement.

À tu galant ché tus m'espouzos
À tu galant ché tus m'espouzos
J'en té ferai rixé marxand
Trin-tran-laboureuse
J'en té ferai rixé marxand
Trin-tran-laboureusement.

Mé yen n'espouzis pas la Biéllos
Mé yen n'espouzis pas la Biéllos
Sans savoir si elles ont de dents
Trin-tran-laboureuse
Sans savoir si elles ont de dents
Trin-tran-laboureusement.

Et lo Biéllo ché mettet à rire
Et lo Biéllo ché mettet à rire
N'avio que dos dins d'avant
Trin-tran-laboureuse
N'avio que dos dins d'avant
Trin-tran-laboureuse
Et uno fasso rigorango
Et l'atrone barabin baraman
Trin-tran-laboureusement.

Mé yen n'espouzis pas la Biéllos
Mé yen n'espouzis pas la Biéllos
Sans savoir si elles on d'argent
Trin-tran-laboureuse
Sans savoir si elles on d'argent
Trin-tran-laboureusement.

Et lo Biéllo chenba à lo cabo
Et lo Biéllo chenba à lo cabo
Ne pomtel un groch plen chac d'excuts blancs
Trin-tran-laboureuse
Ne pomtel un groch plen chac d'excuts blancs
Trin-tran-laboureusement.

Et lou dimenxe feren nocos
Et lou dimenxe feren nocos
Et à lundi l'enterrement
Trin-tran-laboureuse
Et à lundi l'enterrement
Trin-tran-laboureusement.

> Aubé l'arxin d'aquello Biéllo
> Aubé l'arxin d'aquello Biéllo
> J'en aurai une de quinze ans
> Trin-tran-laboureuse
> J'en aurai une de quinze ans
> Trin-tran-laboureusement.

"In Paris there is an old woman who is at least eighty years old.
On Sunday at the church, she seats herself by a fine young man.
' Oh, fine young man, if you'll marry me, I'll make you a rich merchant.'
' I don't marry an old woman without knowing if she has any teeth ! '
The old woman began to laugh, she had two front teeth, and the
One went rigorango, and the other barabin baraman.
' I don't marry an old woman without knowing if she has any money.'
The old woman goes to the cellar and brings up a great full sack of silver pieces.
And on Sunday was the wedding, and on Monday the funeral,
' With the money of that old woman, I'll get a girl who is fifteen years old.' "

Not, perhaps, the best of taste on the part of the *garde champêtre*, you will say, to sing that song.

The angle of the French village on marriage must, in truth, be considered as mercenary. This was vividly illustrated by two incidents which occurred closely one to another.

A young woman was married and had lived with her husband in the house of her father-in-law. A child was born, after which the husband died. The young widow continued to remain in the house of her father-in-law, and in time produced three more children. It was not well thought of, naturally ; but as far as we could learn no *strong* disapproval was shown. The old man, however, now chose to exercise rights which are permitted in France : he legally recognized the last three children as his own. This flung the village into consternation. " The same children are brothers and uncles," gasped the gossips. " *How will they arrange the inheritance ?* "

The second case concerned the son of the village lawyer. He had been successful as a barrister and was now appointed " Chief Prosecutor " at the capital of another province.

For some while he had had a liaison with a divorced woman whose birthplace was this same capital. Situated as he was he could not take her back to her own town. So the Chief Prosecutor married his ex-mistress and brought her to Janac on a tardy honeymoon. The village was scandalized, much more scandalized than by the preceding case.

"Marry a divorced woman!" they ejaculated. "It's unheard of. Why, with his position as Chief Prosecutor, he could have done much better for himself; he might have married *anybody*."

* * *

Undoubtedly money plays a large part in the peasant's life, if only because money accumulates so slowly in his stocking. A farm used to represent a living for the family working it, but the end of the year left no such profits as would help to lessen a respect for the hard cash. Avaricious these peasants are not; for cases of avarice were much discussed. There were, for instance, the three farmers, nicknamed respectively the Wolf, the Lawyer, and the He-goat, who were especially quoted on account of meanness. The Lawyer was put down a well for his pains. The Wolf was also notorious for his toughness of grain. Having been ordered to bed by the doctor, his clothes having been taken away by his daughter, he was discovered on the next morning ploughing his fields stark naked. The He-goat, though reputed wealthy, lived in the woods like a wild man, letting his lands go to rack and ruin because he would expend no money on their cultivation.

A game which tours the local fairs takes advantage of some of the characteristics of the peasants. The game consists of a ball on a string, and the problem is to swing the ball round a peg so that it will swing back into a company

LIFE AND CUSTOMS   109

of ninepins. The prizes were generous, and the game looked simple; the professional manipulator winning at every swing. But to do so depends upon releasing the ball with great calmness and precision; the peasant competitors, partly in eagerness, partly in bashfulness, almost always jerk the ball so that it swings wide.

All the Cheap Jacks and the swindlers play upon the peasant's three characteristics, his suspiciousness, his confidence in his own slyness, and his love of a bargain, his desire to get money for nothing and his belief that everyone else is trying to get his money for nothing. Madame Perigou, the ex-nun, was cheated the other day. A travelling swindler boasted about some shares he had acquired which paid him twelve per cent. He allowed himself with difficulty to be persuaded by Madame Perigou to let her take a large share in the company; it was bankrupt within six months. She lost 10,000 francs.

A farmer went to a Francheville bank to deposit money. The banker himself was reluctant to accept the deposit; urged the farmer not to invest in the bank. The farmer, convinced that he was being kept out of something good, insisted, persisted. His deposit was at last taken. The bank stopped payment next day. He lost 6000 francs.

Vain shrewdness, covetousness, suspicion and self-satisfaction, in a more or less marked measure, seem to be the invariable background of all peasant character; at any rate, they are the characteristics which are so strong that every Reformer must take them into account if his plan is not to be ruined on the rock of Peasantry.

Sestrol had an anecdote, one of his favourites, which cast yet more light on peasant mentality, as well as

on Sestrol's own attitude to life. The performer of it, victim at last to his own ingenuity, was the man who the most moved Sestrol's admiration: himself "*débrouillard*," as he said, he rejoiced over examples of a smarter slyness even though that slyness wrought at last catastrophe.

An ingenious labourer devised the idea of hiring himself out upon the following plan. He offered the farmer to take the following wages, (an old mathematical problem): one grain of wheat for the first day's work, two grains for the second day, four grains for the third, and so on, the sum doubling itself on every successive day. The farmer, staggered at paying in *grains* of corn—believing, first, that he had to deal with a madman, then, with a fool—closed the contract with haste, and learned to repent at leisure. After a few months they began to calculate his wages. They counted the grains in a litre measure of wheat, but litres grew rapidly into sacks, sacks into barnfuls.* . . . The staggered farmer found himself owing a fortune. The case was taken before the *juge de paix*, but the contract was valid. Eventually the farmer was released after paying a heavy commutation.

This trick the wily fellow repeated in several parts of the country.

At last, however, he overreached himself. At the market

* Estimating roughly 70,000 grains of corn to the litre, at the end of sixteen days the labourer had earned one litre of corn, at the end of twenty-three days a sack of 100 litres, while at the end of a month and a half he would have earned no less than four million or more sacks.

of Carmaux he sold three turkeys, demanding one centime for the first toe, two centimes for the second, four for the third, and so on. Three turkeys have twenty-four toes, and the one centime doubling itself for twenty-four times comes to the sum total of one hundred and sixty-seven thousand five hundred and twenty-two francs, fifteen centimes. The case was disputed, but unless my arithmetic is very shaky the fact was indisputable. Eventually the buyers compromised for a thousand francs.

A week later the too clever peasant was found on the road between Cordes and La Vaour with his head beaten in. The murderer was not discovered: truth to tell, I heard the general verdict was that of the *Ingoldsby Legends*, " Sarve him right."

* * *

We did not have many wanderers in Janac. On the whole of our previous walking tour of fifteen days we only met two parties of gipsies: one of French descent, evilly visaged mountebanks with a vagrant cinema; the others Spanish, sellers of smuggled lace and basket makers. To our surprise we discovered that these latter had forgotten much of their own speech. They had been ten years or so in France, had joined up with women of the country—who, however, wore Spanish costume for effect—and now spoke French and several varieties of Southern patois better than their native tongue. They offered to carry our knapsacks in their caravans, but after one glance into the interior we decided that, if it were possible that we would not receive back all the goods we had deposited, we were almost sure to find additions for which we would be by no means thankful. Indeed, the domestic exercise of hunting lice in the hair, at which two women were mutually occupied when we came

112   PEASANTS AND VILLAGERS—

upon them, was in itself a quite sufficient deterrent from accepting the perhaps kindly meant offer.

One cheery couple of tramps, however, arrived in Janac to the joy of the bootmaker's children. They were a man and a woman pushing a small packing case on perambulator wheels, who, greeted pleasantly by all, were evidently well known in the village. They came to the Hôtel Sestrol and

THE UMBRELLA MENDERS.

demanded permission to camp out in the stable as was their yearly habit, but Madame Sestrol had the stable occupied with her flock of little *ritous*, so the vagrants found an old empty house in the distant part of Janac near to the church. They were china and umbrella menders, dog fanciers, fishermen and devotees of Bacchus, and the woman had in earlier years been a circus performer, though nobody would have inferred a past suppleness from her present slouching, angular gait. They were counted as respectable, but their two latter passions swallowed up what profits accrued from their two former pursuits. They were migrating birds, following the climatic changes up and down France, thus dispensing with the necessities of a home. All their worldly possessions could be packed into a wooden box two feet by one foot six and two feet deep. Yet they were happy. They had proved that the only way to possess all one desires is to desire little or nothing. As vagabonds, they had to carry a large waybook which was stamped by the police at every stopping-place. The woman complained that the sergeant at Janac was very insulting and authoritative.

Another vagrant, an irregular visitor and a queer one, was the spoon caster. He sat himself in the shadow of the acacias by the Hôtel Sestrol, set up a small charcoal hearth, brought out an old iron frying-pan and sundry strange blocks of metal, the spoon moulds. To him came out Madame Sestrol with an apronful of the debris of pewter spoons. It appears that the pewter spoon is a sore temptation to the peasant in his cups, he shows off feats of finger strength upon it. The broken pewter spoons were now put into the frying-pan; the charcoal was blown up to brightness; the craftsman clapped a mould between his knees, and in a few minutes Madame Sestrol's grey-looking rubbish heap was converted into new spoons, seven large and a dozen small ones, bright and silvery.

The Cheap Jack photographer is also abroad. He now makes a victim of those parents who have lost sons during the war; he offers to do them enlargements of their son's picture for nothing—he says as an advertisement in the locality—which offer, tempting the peasant greed, makes the parent sign a paper couched in ambiguous terms, by which he finds, to his amazement and disgust, that he has bound himself to pay for a most expensive frame. A typical way of diddling the peasant this.

**

Nothing could have been more pleasant than the behaviour of the villagers and of the peasantry to ourselves. Courtesy and friendliness were shown on every hand, especially in our own section of the village. The faubourg was colder to us, and there one girl sniggered at Jo's painting. But the faubourg was reputedly cold and unwelcoming. Even though we heard that some busybodies in the lower village had got up the usual spy scare, we could never guess from behaviour who were the agitators. The reason for this spy rumour was amusing; the more observant said, " These people call themselves painters, but every painter who comes here paints the old Gateway and Hippolyte's pigeon-loft: these people have painted neither the old Gateway nor Hippolyte's pigeon-loft, *ergo*, they are not genuine painters."

Some persons *did* insinuate that the way of the stranger was easy, that the villager himself suffered from the scandal, tittle-tattle and jealousies incident to village life; that the stranger bringing a hint of novelty was welcome—for a time. All this is probably true. Still, one may put down one fact which has struck us, which is that amongst the European countries we have visited France seems the most free on the *social* level; a person who wishes to live his life in his own way is here the most freed from weight of criticism and oppression of convention. And as the property-owning peasant is possibly the freest person in the community, so the peasant Frenchman is possibly the freest man in the world. There still remains in France some tinge of the old Roman spirit, it is the last of the classicists.

Another noticeable feature of the French peasant is his readiness for intelligent discussion. Sestrol may fight us off with his " *chacun son métier*," but he is merely repudiating information which he does not feel capable of absorbing. A discussion is another affair. The Frenchman, no matter what his station, loves the *play* of the mind ; I will not say as much for village women, the household-factory soon atrophies them. Nevertheless, one must keep off politics. Politics, which could be, are never allowed to be, an exercise of the mind : they remain always mere assertion, the hobby of the egoistical in man.

VI

EATERS AND EATEN, AND GASTRONOMIC THINGS

WE lunch, as we breakfast, out of doors in a more leisurely fashion at our normal hour after the hurry of the peasant diners has died down, while the farmers are arguing over their cognac-flavoured coffee.

Over against where we sit at table is the hole in the wall which is Tuk-Tuk's front door. It is placed some four feet from the cobbled gutter and a primitive ladder made of slats nailed across a pole, a ladder of which many of the slats are missing, others awry, affords a precarious method of mounting from the street. Still, Tuk-Tuk, being a cockerel, has an excellent sense of balance, and no laxity on the part of the human owners disturbs his ingress or egress from the hen-house. The hen-house itself is no mere hen-house. It is the corner of a human house, itself the corner of the triangular *place*. Nor is the hen-house only a hen-house, it is a small room on the ground floor, unlighted and unventilated except for the hole of about the size of a brick, Tuk-Tuk's front door, but in this room are housed a colony of rabbits enclosed in a barrel and a hutch of young and staggering ducks.

The roof of Tuk-Tuk's residence makes a flat narrow terrace enclosed by a balcony of old and beautiful ironwork and shaded by a thick pergola in which the grapes are already in the greyish transition between green and purple, and all about the pergola the house is stained a fine blue-green with the copper sulphate spraying of the vines, sprayings intended to keep off the green fly and other pests which the country-people assert are deposited by mist. We face Tuk-Tuk's front door across the street, that street debouching from the triangular *place* at the corner, so that, just round the corner, the other door leading into the basement or *basse-cour* of the house is full in the *place* itself, the whole of which we can see from our dining-table beneath the acacia trees.

This other door to the house of the owners of Tuk-Tuk is a semi-submerged door; you go down to it by a series of steps, for the *place* itself lies at a steep angle, so that the Romanly-arched lintel of the door is on a level with your knees; and as we sit at our table tasting the first mouthfuls of Madame Sestrol's excellent *soupe* tinged with a dash or two of *pinard*, we watch this door with some anxiety. Indeed, the full enjoyment of our meal is delayed until that door has opened, we finish our *soupe* with its sodden bread-crusts, we eat our bread, we pour out glasses of red *pinard*— of the red wine brought in casks from the slopes to the north of Gaillac—we eat our fresh-river trout from the Aveyron, trout with a faint flavour of the soil tinging its harmonious flesh; but all these delights are minimized in value if that Sphynx of a door has not delivered up its daily secret. Tuk-Tuk and Kissme, little Faust and Mimi are usually about our feet, but we give them only a half attention until the query of the door has been solved. Or rather, it depends. If the wind was from the west, we used not to give the door a thought—we enjoyed our *soupe*, our *pinard*, our trout to its most delicious full; but if the wind was easterly, or if it hung with the heavy languorous stillness of a breathless midsummer, why, then, this door was Fate for us.

* * *

As we sit eating our trout, while Tuk-Tuk on the one side and Mimi on the other come expectantly for morsels inedible by man, an ox-cart loaded with faggots comes along.

We are in the period after the harvest and immediately before the vine gathering. The flails are still whirling in the cobbled streets, and a primitive threshing engine has

THE FLAILERS.

just ceased its dusty moan on the common-land opposite the chemist's house. The corn is carried to the baker, who credits the owner with so much bread in exchange, so many loaves per sack. The peasants have little else to do now but to draw in from their woods a supply of fuel for the winter, coal being rarely used in Janac. The cart comes groaning as though it has rheumatism in its joints ; it moves almost with the careful air of the rheumatic. Before it the serious oxen step with deliberation, turning out their forefeet as though they had been trained by a Victorian dancing-master ; their patient, reproachful eyes are invisible, for as the weather is hot they wear, against the flies, veils of closely woven string, mussul-women amongst animals. They go, yoked head to head, with horns interlocked under a great wooden bond which unites them more rigorously than does the marriage service, for practically the only part left free from this communism is the tail. Before the oxen strolls the driver, or rather leader, Raymond's rejected, who lounges on with what appears to be the gait of a girl bored with life, but which is in reality from habit calculated to the exact paces of her deliberate beasts. Over her shoulder she carries a long hazel wand and from time to time she leans back with a graceful slow gesture and with the rod touches the yoke between the oxen, thus intimating to the beasts that their road is still straightforward. At any turn she indicates the direction by the movement of her rod as though she were steering a ship by the bows. She gives us smile and nod as the tower of brushwood moves by us, sweeping down from the acacia trees a shower of leaves which Tuk-Tuk would swallow in default of further fishbones or pellets of bread, and for which the clumsy ducks of Madame Sestrol used to waddle out of the artificial pool which our good hostess has contrived by a dam across the opposite gutter and a few pailfuls of water. The ox-cart goes slowly across the triangular *place* and then has to contrive to swing around into the narrow road steeply descending from the lower corner. The ox-girl makes uncouth noises to her beasts, she steers them well out ere she gives with the long wand that angular movement which makes the right-hand ox pivot outwards and which makes the old cart groan as though afflicted with a hundred torments. As soon as they feel the slope the oxen move with yet greater care : the whole weight of the cart is now upon their foreheads, their massive necks quiver with the strain, the vibration of the cart on the cobbles is transmitted through the shaft-pole and through the wooden yoke directly to their brain pans ; if they had headaches, would this gigantic vibrant massage cure the ill, I wonder, this vibrator of half a ton playing on the cerebellum ?

The villagers hereabouts, in Languedoc, cannot understand or even mentally picture an oxenless England, they cannot imagine how without draught cattle farming is to be done. To see sleek kine standing lazily in the lush grass, cows which have no purpose other than that of transforming chlorophyll and carbohydrates into proteids and fats, would shock them profoundly. " Fainéant," they would call *them*, as we have said they dub us or anybody who does not labour with hoe or with fork, anybody who is not bent under the Adamite curse in the most obvious way. The Southern Frenchman seems, in truth, rather too excitable to use horses for rough work, he can manœuvre the slow ox in complex situations, he can shout a panic at his will, the ox has no nerves, but the average Southern farmer would have his horses as hysterical as are his dogs if he were set to handle them over difficult country ; here horses are for the roads, and even so but one man in the village ventures to drive them in a team. Yet, though the ox is methodical and apparently not unintelligent to work with, he is a problem to shoe. I think, like so many otherwise phlegmatic persons, he must be ticklish : at any rate, a whole elaborate apparatus, a sort of ox-dock, is needed to fit him for the road. A stout erection of solid beams receives his body, and in it he is

AND GASTRONOMIC THINGS 121

hoisted and strapped immovably in every part, except his alarmed tail which, often weighted with dung, remains a formidable mace ready to welt an incautious blacksmith over the head, an unsavoury weapon. The ox has eight shoes, two for each foot, since it is cloven. The irons are almond-shaped with tongues which are bent over the point

THE OX-DOCK.

of the hoof. They are fixed by nails to the outside of the hoof only, and the tongue slipping up through the cleft is bent over the horn to hold the iron in place. In Serbia they use no such elaborate gallows for shoeing the oxen, they tether the animal's legs to a heavy beam, roll him over on to his back, and so have the hoofs presented upwards most conveniently for work. The primitive may often be an improvement upon the sophisticated.

* * *

Madame Sestrol comes out with a plate of chicken and tomatoes fried in goose grease and lard.

Madame Sestrol, dear soul, watches us attack the veal with lines of anxiety wrinkling her brow. She can never be quite convinced that we can eat goose-grease cooking, being, on the other hand, quite incredulous that anybody can honestly like any other. France is divided into three culinary zones, the torrid, the temperate and the frigid zones, as it were, of gastronomy; these regions are the oil, the grease and the butter provinces. Madame Sestrol has learned that there are people who say that they prefer things cooked in butter to things cooked in lard or goose grease, but it is knowledge without comprehension, just as she has learned that people in the Antipodes are standing on their heads relatively to herself. So though she is half aware that grease cooking may not be our natural diet, she says with a grimace of disgust, " You can't like that horrible cooking in butter, faugh!" or " I can't stomach oil, can you ?" Just as Raymond—good-natured but tactless—can understand that we should have a prejudice in favour of our own countrymen, but does not expect us seriously to contradict his assertion that in the war " one French *poilu* was as good as any two Englishmen."

Your Northern Frenchman would almost come to blows with the Southern over the virtues of the respective bases of the kitchen. We have, after three months of laudatory speeches, almost convinced Madame Sestrol that cooking in grease is not distasteful to us—as she cooks, that is— but we have never, never dared to hint to her that yet another cookery school exists, the English or water school. It is true that Madame Sestrol will serve *bouilli* with all the goodness diffused into the *soupe*, only the fibre being left; this we munch with gherkins, more as a duty than as a pleasure, to save her from disappointment. But if we had revealed that the English boil beef and mutton for the meat, that we boil vegetables—such as green peas, French beans, cabbage or brussels sprouts—and serve up the result unjumped in the frying-pan, or undecorated with sauce, her opinion of us—which is high now—might drop to irrecoverable depths. One day we shook her credulity to its foundation by saying in England one eats red-currant jelly with mutton. She could bear the fact that we were heretics—repudiating, as they assert bluntly, the Blessed Virgin—but, if we had *insisted* that mutton and jelly make a delectable culinary combination, I am convinced that Madame Sestrol would have given us notice to quit. As it was, we contrived to leave her with the impression that we were merely deploring the gastronomic barbarities of our fellow-countrymen.

And we *had* to mind our P's and Q's. Tact was the order of the day. It isn't every week in these post-war conditions that one can discover in a queer, old, almost mediæval village in France, such a place as we had discovered in the Hôtel Sestrol. We were not going to get ourselves pushed out of clover like this just on account of a difference about the tasty harmonies of jelly with mutton. And with a Southern Frenchman one has to be careful; from jelly and mutton to the Ruhr might only be the work of a few sentences, things being ticklish just then about them. The *Dépêche*, the local paper, had some very cutting things to say about England, which we hoped to live down by personal charm: is not example more powerful than precept?

But to return to Madame Sestrol's immediate anxiety, we were beginning to pick a bit at our meat. You can't expect everything for ten francs a day, which with the exchange at 75 equalled about 2s. 9½d. We had not, indeed, expected as much as we got. *Soupe*, trout, chicken and tomatoes, to be followed by custard; by Roquefort cheese (real creamy Roquefort, not the dried mummy of Roquefort which reaches England) or by small fresh country cheeses brought in on bay leaves, *Cantaloupe* melon, and then coffee with a dash of cognac make a fair meal for a *pensionnaire* at two and ninepence odd per day. They had warned us that we would only get country fare, but this was a good average sample, besides, I have forgotten the wine. Red country wine *ad lib*. Clearly Monsieur and Madame Sestrol—who have some reputation in the village, having clambered to their present state solely by their own efforts—must have been caught napping when they made so absurd a bargain. But they don't seem to repine. Madame Sestrol grumbles not because we eat up her profits but because we don't eat enough of them. Yet we are beginning to pick at our meat, we are beginning to be what parents call in children "dainty."

We are Broad Church in this cooking quarrel, we will eat your oil, butter, lard or goose-grease, nor will we repudiate peas steamed with a sprig of mint for the delights of any orthodoxy.* But we confess to two things, one, that after several months of the hottest French midsummer the invariable fried meat, whether composed of veal or mutton, of chicken or of rabbit (even of partridge, at ten francs a day!) begins to pall—it does seem to us after serious trial that goose grease is probably more consistently

---

* Though we are ready to admit that the virtue of boiled cabbage or of boiled potatoes can, like any other virtue, become insipid with time if too much in evidence.

delectable as a winter diet—
secondly, that the foregoing list
lacks one important item,
beef. Beef is a rarity for the
French village-dweller, at least
in these parts of Languedoc;
eat beef, why, it would be like
eating your traction-engine.
But the interdiction upon beef
springs from no sad sentiment,
peasants aren't sentimental
about animals. It is a question
of bulk. The village butcher
dare risk no slaughter of a
whole ox unless upon some
very special occasion. A calf
he can dispose of in a week,

and more rarely a sheep, but even these meats are not too
readily bought; the French peasant eats his bread by
the joint, his meat in veritable tea-table fingers, besides,
has he not his *basse-cour* running with chickens and
his cellar corners crowded with rabbit hutches in which
the furry victims seldom see the day till that of their
extinction. The butcher in Janac is far less prosperous
than the baker. I confess that after so many months
we crave for beef, we crave for a bit o' steak done rare,
for something with the juice running out. A fig for
your anæmic fleshes. I would have a law interdicting the
slaughter of calves as detrimental to the health of the nation.
It is only since we have marked upon ourselves the effect
of too much veal that we have become truly observant of
the complexions of the villagers. They are meridionals.
Not so dark-haired maybe as you might expect; still, they

hold to the darker side of complexion, all except the granddaughter of the owner of Tuk-Tuk, a child who is silver-gilt like a thing translucent to the sunlight. Now, meridional people after three months of sunning should be almost of an Indian tint. These are browned, but beneath this surface tanning there shows a pallor due to lack of blood. There is a bloodless air about the place, many of the young girls, too, suffer from chlorosis.

***

Of these varied meats which do not compensate us for the lack of beef, Tuk-Tuk prefers chicken, he is cannibal. Tuk-Tuk is, as I have said, a cockerel, but has this peculiarity, he is a regular Dempsey amongst cockerels. We have watched him grow. His first experience of life would stand as a terrible lesson to all strict Americans. At the age of three hours he was made drunk, he rolled on his back, he turned up his toes in infantile tipsiness. It is the custom here to give white wine to the first hatched chickens in order to keep them drunkenly quiet till the reluctant hatchers can ooze from the egg. I'll bet that Tuk-Tuk was sprightly enough as a hatcher.

We remember his first fight when he stood looking rather like a ruffled toy feather duster on two sticks opposed to an equally ruffled, equally toy duster; each frozen into belligerent stiffness, each waiting for an opening. Tuk-Tuk's subsequent battles in the triangular *place* mount into hundreds during a few months. We remember his first crow, when, his little neck stretched upwards as though he were being lynched by an invisible halter, he uttered what was meant for a clarion note but which sounded very like the scrape of a slate pencil mishandled by a vicious schoolboy. Tuk-Tuk became Jo's pupil as Mimi was mine. She taught him to jump for morsels held in the fingers, and we came to estimate his preferences by the heights to which he would spring for the tit-bit. It was not, indeed, a spring without risks. Mimi the cat, Kissme the dog, little Faust the pup, hung about us as eagerly as did Tuk-Tuk himself. The latter launching himself upwards to snatch from Jo's fingers the coveted dainty could not always be sure that he might

TUK-TUK.

not descend unwittingly upon the fearful backs of his competitors, Mimi of the claws or Kissme of the teeth. Placed together all three on the level, neither Mimi nor Kissme would have dared to offer injury to Tuk-Tuk, they respected property ; but what if this property were to descend suddenly and whirling, flutter on to their backs ? They were both nervous animals, the actions of fright are often made without reflection. For chicken Tuk-Tuk would brave the adventurous leap of some four feet vertically, for lesser meats but three feet six or so, soft bread tempted him to three feet on hungry days, crust he would not deign to consider. The thing which most astonished us was the power of his eyesight. He could distinguish at once what was and what was not a prize worth the effort, and we seldom saw him jump mistaking dross for gold. But if I am to be incarnated I hope that my manifest sins do not condemn me to become chicken during my next avatar. To Mimi, Kissme or little Faust meal-time was a precarious moment, a morsel had to be simultaneously eaten and defended, or had to be flown with to some secret banqueting cell; but Tuk-Tuk once having snatched his morsel from Jo's fingers then enjoyed a meal which was more than three-quarters Marathon. The tit-bit once fairly embeaked a crowd of envious fowl would swoop upon him; off he would dash with a leggy stride, he would dip and dodge like a clever three-quarter getting through the enemy's scrum, but, alas, no goal line was there for him, nowhere could he touch down with safety. It is awkward enough dining when your hand and your mouth are the same utensil, but it becomes a torture when a host of greedy hand-mouths are waiting to rip away your prize. Tuk-Tuk perhaps got his dinner at about three pecks per hundred yards. Pray Buddha I don't become a hen.

* *
 *

Jo was preserving on the edge of her plate several delectable morsels of chicken for Tuk-Tuk. To-day he will leap at least four feet. But no Tuk-Tuk appears. Now and then he is thus absent, sometimes seduced to the lower streets in search of oddments, sometimes shut up in the hen-house with the rabbits.

Madame Sestrol comes to change our plates.

AND GASTRONOMIC THINGS

" What a pity Tuk-Tuk is not here," says my wife, " I have saved some especial bits for him."

" What do you mean ? " asks our hostess, wrinkling her brows.

" Why," returns Jo, " the cockerel which I have taught to jump so cleverly. You know, the brown one with the large comb."

" Eh ? " says Madame Sestrol. " The brown one ? Oh yes, he who used to jump. *Eh bien!* He is there."

And she points dramatically to Jo's plate.

Poor Tuk-Tuk. I don't think we would have eaten him if we had been warned beforehand, but, alas, the deed is done, Tuk-Tuk has taken his promotion in the scale of nature. But Tuk-Tuk has left in me one poignant memory. Have you ever looked a hen full closely in the face ? I do not know any sight more packed with concentrated suggestion of the grotesque and the evil than the near sight of a hen's countenance. I try to picture myself a worm to feel the whole terror of that awful thing approaching. It is almost unimaginable. But if, as the old hymn said, " Worms have learned to lisp Thy name," what strange sounds must they not produce when a Nemesis so monstrous, so grim-visaged hovers over them !

* * *

I think also that I'd rather not become a cat in a French village. Not that Mimi receives active ill-treatment. I don't think that anybody *could* ill-treat Mimi, she is the soul of elusion. Visually she is a black cat with sloping hindquarters ; orally she is also ; but tangibly she does not exist. At least she does not exist tangibly to us, stretch we our hand ever so cautiously, she is a millimetre beyond our finger-tips ; but she is tangible enough to Kissme and to little Faust who utter nerve-racking yells from beneath

 our table whenever in some question of reparations Mimi plants her claws into the others' tender noses. We are apt to look upon cats as domesticated animals, but I wonder. In England maybe the cat is now a domesticated animal, but after having lived in France and Spain, especially in the country districts, I'm not sure of the true status of the cat. I think that the cat is only just becoming a domesticated animal, previously it was but tolerated vermin allowed to prey upon rats and mice, the intolerable vermin. Kipling's *Just So* story is all wrong even in Europe to-day.

Nor do I wish to be incarnated a French village dog. Kissme and little Faust are French village dogs. You may think that the names are invented by a whimsical author, but they are exactly as we found them. Raymond knew beforehand that Kissme was an English word though its significance surprised him. How the pup became Faust is a problem. We asked the reason, but no hint of the legend nor yet of the play or of the opera has filtered through to Janac. " *C'est un nom du chien, quoi?* " replied Raymond. Faust, prototype of the soul seller, hero for Marlowe and for Goethe, inspiration for Berlioz and for Gounod, has come to be a mere " *nom du chien.*" It's as bad as:

> " Imperial Cæsar, dead and turned to clay,
> Will stop a hole to keep the draught away."

Kissme is anything but her name, except when there is food to be coaxed. She is a little, brown, wriggling, lunar-eyed, cringing, yapping, obnoxious piece of dogflesh called generally "*un rattier*." The true territory of the hotel ceases at the edge of the pavement which they rent from the village *placier* for 30 francs a year, but Kissme, like David Copperfield's aunt, has extended a claim over three parts of the road which lies before the house. No donkeys on the sacred sward were ever assailed by Miss Trotwood with more energy than Kissme assails anything moving which encroaches within this territory: oxen, horses, dogs, motor-cars, chickens, ducks, children, donkeys and pigs are saluted with ear-splitting objections, in which Kissme has a Janet represented by little Faust. The Southern races have no nerves for noise, the thready shrillings of these two animals almost rip the drum of the ear, but no correction is ever applied. Indeed, we are reminded of a conversation overheard in the train. A French soldier returning from the Ruhr was discussing Germany. What had struck him most of all was that the German trains left the station without whistling, he was speaking of some important terminus.

"But I tell you," he added proudly, "we soon altered that. We had a fine racket going on in no time. Why, it wasn't like a proper railway station before!"

Correction when it does come, however, is handed out only too generously, almost in a Sodom and Gomorrah fashion. Little Faust having lived for some three months picking up all his mother's bad habits, acquiring one or two of his own, suddenly, the other day, transgressed the limits. It happened that the wife of the blacksmith, a pessimistic woman, had turned loose a bevy of young ducks into the road. Little Faust, with no education, saw these rolling, peeping things—*ritous*—as playthings loosed for his benefit. He cornered one in a filthy yard protected from the street by a gate of iron grille, and here in safety he proceeded to test the virtues of his needle teeth. The shrieks of the blacksmith's wife called Raymond on to the scene: the duckling was rescued. Faust then was *taught*. Raymond, of course, lost his temper and we had literally to drag him from the puppy which could just creep away. But the animal's trials were not yet over, for Monsieur Sestrol, a very kind-hearted man in general, coming on the scene and learning of the enormity, reflogged the pup so callously that for half an hour afterwards it lay on the ground incapable of movement, after which it crawled to some dark hole to wonder what had happened, for no attempt had been made to connect crime and punishment in the animal's consciousness. The blacksmith's wife, mourning over its sad fate, held in her hand the injured duckling; it was but a week or so old, and looked, to all intents and purposes, dead. The head hung down, the legs were up, the eyes were hidden by ghastly leaden-coloured lids. And then in a tearful voice the woman began again to explain the tragedy to us.

"He squeezed it thus," exclaimed the blacksmith's wife, forgetting herself in the energy of her interpretations and squeezing the unfortunate duckling till one could almost hear its bones crack. "It was too dreadful. He shook it so," she cried pitifully, jerking the unconscious animal to and fro with a vicious movement. Whatever it had suffered from little Faust it suffered over again in the blacksmith's wife's too poignant illustrations. Then having done her best to extinguish what sparks of life yet remained, she gave it a dose of strong coffee and hoped for the best. Marvellous to tell, both the duckling and little Faust survived.

The other day Monsieur Sestrol propounded this question to us, " Why is it in the nature of the dog to snap at and bite human beings, especially postmen ? " which sufficiently illustrates the attitude of dog to man or rather of man to dog in these lands, for the dog is but what man makes him. Indeed, it is unpleasant to go for country walks since at every turn one is greeted by some yapping, snarling cur which renders the air clamorous with his barking. The dogs  of the village, too, are the weirdest assortment of mongrels that it has ever been my fate to see, and once more Monsieur Sestrol asked, " Have you got dogs like these in England ? " Had we spoken truthfully we would have retorted, " In England a set of dogs like this would be hurried off to the lethal chamber at once." But he could not have understood. Cows merely for milk, and ordinary dogs for courage and race lie almost beyond the edge of his not unintelligent peasant mind ; in the French country, dogs are kept to yap, and anything on four legs with a yap will serve.*

But we must not blame the peasant, especially the Southern peasant, because he does not *love* cats and dogs. The sentimental love of animals is a late development of

* Except sporting dogs, of which Janac had several almost valuable specimens.

civilization. Less than a hundred years ago we tolerated slavery. Janac in almost every way is as the Revolution left it; it has electric light, often dim either for lack or surfeit of water, it has an electric breadmixer to save the brawny arms of Cou-Cou the baker's man, it has a steam-threshing machine; it had breech-loading shot-guns with which to massacre the red-legged patridge, and the *sauvage* rabbit, but in most other respects it is eighteenth or even seventeenth century. Besides, it is difficult to love dogs and cats in a land where inevitably they are swarming with fleas; the most tender, already active sentiment here hesitates to express itself, so how is sentiment yet unawakened to arise with so lively a deterrent? The dogs here certainly have no leisure to "brood over being dogs" as David Harum says.

There is one donkey which Kissme hates as sincerely as Miss Trotwood hated the whole species, it is a large and solemn animal named Tambour, about as big as a mule, a giant of a donkey. Tambour, hated by Kissme for some unaccountable reason, is well treated, but not appreciated by his owners, who keep the village shop. These people, with the baker and the shoemaker St. Mouxa—do not confound the latter with the *épicier*-cobbler—are the only tradesmen in the village whom one should not call amateur tradesmen, that is, they are the only people who live and expect to make full money by their trades. The owner of Tambour has a real shop—that is to say, lives by it: St. Mouxa has a real shop. Poor Tambour, however, is unappreciated. His master considers the donkey as a blot on his escutcheon. The man was once a policeman, and his now portly dignity would feel itself fitted with nothing less than a horse; though Tambour does twice the work a horse of his value could perform. But ambition stifles dignity.

AND GASTRONOMIC THINGS

Tambour is kept because these people have greater dreams yet. They have their eyes on Paris; Paris which is sucking the best blood from the villages, which takes the rough peasant, in one generation turning him into a *bon bourgeois*, in two transforming the rough-hewn  stock of the soil into the courteous doctor or the smooth-tongued *avocat*. Tambour's owners have done so well by sticking to one business that they meditate selling it and making a raid on the Capital.

* *
*

The ducks of Madame Sestrol, having enjoyed during the hot morning the delights of their fabricated pool and having practically emptied it of water, are now quacking loudly for their food. They know and love Madame Sestrol, while she has an equal affection for them, though I fear it is but cupboard love on both sides. But for her side of the matter Madame Sestrol shows an aspect of humanity which never fails to puzzle me. The chief nourishment for ducks in Janac consists of nettle leaves, chopped up finely. Every morning, for three months at least, Madame Sestrol has sought for, gathered and chopped up nettles. Nor is she the only one: the tobacconist's daughter chops nettles as does the blacksmith's wife. These people go hunting the nettle, ·each has her secret spot where the vegetable grows thickly. Every duck in the village represents at least three months of stung and swollen hands, for of course the peasant would not deign to wear gloves. *Well*, balancing up the pain of nettle-cutting against the joys of duck eating, I confess that nine dinners of duck would not compensate me for a hundred days of nettle-stung hands; and in like manner it so often appears to me that a full two-thirds of the pleasures which humanity scrambles after do little to balance the labour and pains of providing the means of enjoyment.

But doom, not in cloudy shape indeed, but in the generous form of Madame Sestrol, hung over the ducks. We had duck for dinner two days ago; fat duck. There came a day when Madame Sestrol desisted from her nettle hunts. She selected five of the ducks, the plumpest, cut a snip out of their

CUPBOARD LOVE ON BOTH SIDES.

crests for identification, and then . . . the process of stuffing began. Gripping a bird between her knees she introduced a tin funnel into its protesting throat, and by slow degrees poured maize into its crop, with copious draughts of water. The ducks "swelled wisibly." Their livers degenerated with delectable rapidity.

Fat enough and diseased enough at last they went into one of the burnished copper cauldrons and were reduced to grease, a substitute for goose grease, though the liver is not counted so good, nor has it the lasting qualities of goose liver.

Madame Sestrol said that the ducks became cognizant of their fate and that invariably the liver of the last duck killed of a flock has gone green with fright. She also told us that ducks' eggs, like blackberries, are often considered poisonous by the country people.

And now at last, prolonged sufficiently to overshadow the whole of our meal, as we are eating our *canteloupe* melon, that Sphynx of a door is opened. That door in the sideways edge of Tuk-Tuk's owner's house, which maybe you have forgotten. A little old woman with a long switch descends the steps, a huge key is turned, she shrills in a cracked voice, "*Ven! Ven! Ven!*" bearing aloft as temptation two cobs of Indian corn richly pearled with golden grains. Staggering up the steps clamber a pair of pigs looking like— coming events casting shadows before—badly made raw sausages. The pigs are not fat; they have suffered with the season. The peasant pig is only a transformer of refuse, a sort of animate incinerator, and so reflects the barrenness of the drought. The peasant does not calculate that so much extra feeding, so many sous' worth of grain can by them be transmuted into so many francs' worth of flesh and fat. The old woman shrieks "*Ven! Ven!*" switching them lustily with her rod. The pigs race down the road, out of nose-shot, thank heavens! We sigh with relief, the pigs having been turned out for exactly the same reason as Tasso, the lady's lap-dog, is run at night in the garden. Most of the village pigs are thus house-trained, each is given its daily airing. We are accustomed to think of the *basse-cour* as the farmyard, but in these villages of peasant proprietorship every house has its *basse-cour*, that *basse-cour* being the basement from which animal effluvia rises through the whole house. Courtesy makes the old woman try to drive her pigs to a distance sufficient not to nauseate us. She, being steeped in them, has no prejudices or objections to animal smells of any sort, but has delicacy enough to respect our idiosyncrasy though she does not understand it. Her old husband is not so intelligent, or maybe he is anti-British. We used to dread the days when 'twas he who let the pigs out.

* * *

Anyway, the villagers think that we are a queer couple. They cannot fathom our interest in animals. Why had we taught Tuk-Tuk to leap for morsels. Why have we taught Kissme the meaning of " Down " ? Kissme, who has never learned a thing in nine years except that when one heavy bump resounds from the kitchen Madame Sestrol is probably trimming meat and there may be scraps to pick up, whereas repeated bumps indicate that she is mincing herbs or stuffing, which has no profit for a dog.

The peasants' attitude towards animals is one of indifference, as a whole. One man loved horses, one boy fondled dogs. But we were surprised to find that Monsieur Sestrol and Raymond each confessed to a *pleasure* in slaying animals, in taking life. How much is the impulse to destroy life inherent in living things ? Do not all carnivorous animals kill for pleasure ? Sestrol admitted, however, to a distaste for killing kids. " They cry so much like little children," he said. Here we see in Sestrol the first beginnings of that feeling which culminates in Buddhism.

VII

THE STRANGE CASE OF MONSIEUR LEMOULE

WE are sipping our coffee after the leisurely lunch; while Madame Sestrol, her hands folded upon the shelf of her stomach, is taking the air with satisfaction after the completed task. She is telling us how the Government inspectors came searching for concealed grain during the War, and how one of the inspectors, electing to sleep with Raymond, put all his clothes on to a chest which was packed full of contraband wheat. Suddenly she interrupts her story, and speaks with a faint accent of irritation:

"Oh! Here is *your* friend, Monsieur Lemoule."

From the lower corner of the triangular *place* comes a young man, dark, stocky, with a small moustache and with active eyes. He limps slightly. Oursa, the black dog, follows him. Poor Oursa, she has been in trouble. Two days ago the family went to the railway station leaving the dog behind. Oursa followed surreptitiously, and crossing the line made a dash for the platform just as the train was coming in. She was overtaken, run down, received a hard blow on the forehead, and half her tail was cut off. To-day, for the first time, she has come out of that dark solitude where animals in pain find some relief. She is going about self-consciously with head on one side, and she finds that there are strange invisible prickles wherever she would sit down: it is pathetically amusing to note the air with which she creeps stealthily along trying to elude that invisible practical joker who stabs at her tail whenever it touches the ground.

Monsieur Gerard Lemoule approaches with a studied carelessness. Both he and we enjoy these after-lunch or after-dinner chats, yet we pretend, chance. He *happens* along, we invite him to sit, Madame Sestrol presses him to take coffee. It is our final talk. We have one or two books to return to him, a copy of Jack London's *Mutiny of the Elsinore;* Octave Mirbeau's *Confessions d'un Homme Sensible*. He gives us back Conrad's *Shadow Line*, which he has enjoyed, and Defoe's *Journal of the Plague Year*, which was a little too difficult for him.

Lemoule is a naturalized American, but, if there is any truth in Mr. Sinclair Lewis's revelations, he is American in nothing but his adopted nationality. Son of a small hotel-keeper in the suburbs of Paris, an Aveyronnais, he profited by education so much that he had learned some English before he left school. He entered life as a commercial clerk : but as commercial clerk saw no outlet. Long hours and poor pay and no chance summed up a future which could not content him. He threw up his position and shipped as a steward on a boat voyaging to South America. When the time for his military service came he found himself a strong anti-militarist and removed himself to an English liner and later to an American. He went ashore in America, becoming a waiter, as which he had an easier life, better pay and better conditions than as a clerk in France. He had long meant to become an American citizen, but had put off the matter.

The War found Lemoule in an awkward position. He had become an enthusiastic pro-American, he had dodged his military duty, but he was still legally a Frenchman. If he returned to France he expected to be put into gaol, after which his position as a returned deserter would be probably uncomfortable. He went to Canada to try to enlist in that country, but Canada would not enlist a French citizen. So in disgust he backed on to his Americanization ; he was, in fact, quite a normal man of vacillating qualms, punctilios, principles and egoisms. He joined the American armies on the Declaration of War by the United States, became an American citizen *de facto*, and went at once  to France. He served till the Armistice, was returned to America, was injured between two lorries shortly after landing, was invalided from the service, and pensioned with what amounts now to about 700 francs a month.

With the dollars, which would equal 700 francs, living in America was impossible : with a damaged pelvis, dropped foot and general disorganization of the nerves of the left leg, Lemoule could not resume his old occupation. He came back to France where 700 francs represents comfort. Unfortunately, the leisure of an assured income after his years of toil gave Lemoule the impression that he could for ever live with complacency the life of a *rentier*, culling with his American money the citizenship and advantages disturbed by none of the drawbacks of France. On a visit to his uncle it was suggested to him that he should take a wife. So in accordance with French custom the village gossips, set to reviewing the marriageable girls, chose Yvonne for him. He and Yvonne having fanned up a high intensity of the amorous, to the order of convenience and of suitability of station, the wedding was happily consummated.* Lemoule settled down in the house of his father-in-law to enjoy what are considered life's greatest benefits, an attractive wife and nothing to do.

But Lemoule did not find that perfect content can be contained within these narrow boundaries, an agreeable wife and a sufficient income. For instance, his position in the village was not wholly comfortable.

We had first become acquainted with Lemoule as he was unharnessing his donkey. The Hôtel Sestrol, lying, like all other Janac houses, on the steep slope of the hill, had stables in the basement half underground. To reach these from the road a narrow, dark, cobbled alley, filthy with manure, led steeply downhill. This alley served also the stables of the cooper-tobacconist and of the baker. We had asked Madame Sestrol some unimportant question which she could not answer; to our surprise a voice speaking good English gave us the needed information. A short conversation elicited the fact that Lemoule had learned his English in America; but he was late for lunch, the conversation was interrupted. The baker, however, took up the tale.

"That fellow," said the baker, "is a *scélérat*."

But first the baker's own story must light up his point of view. The baker is a consumptive, and with that strange optimism inherent in this illness he affirms that he is getting better. "Since I left this fool of a doctor and have gone to Francheville. Young man there, knows all the latest— I'm going to electrical treatment soon." The baker's illness

---

* "Au bout de quatre jours Mme. Lebrument adorait son mari."—GUY DE MAUPASSANT.

is the result of the War. He was captured early during the fighting and imprisoned in Germany.

"*Straff-kommando* all the time for me," he said, in a queer voice like the musical creak of an overloaded waggon. "Augh! I couldn't squat down all the time like a little sheep. If I get angered I do things like this, for instance: unloading pig-iron we were and an Englishman calls me a dirty name—he thought I didn't understand, but I did—so I drops the pig I was carrying on to his foot. Oah yess! And his foot comes off, that's what he got for calling me names.

"Eh! I escaped five times—five times. One night I did get into Switzerland and didn't know it. Went on walking; ended by walking right across the frontier back into Germany again; caught in the morning a mile in—still walking deeper into the *sacré* country. Hard luck, eh?

"Germans harsh? What do you think? They *had* to be harsh, with fellows like me about. All I know is this, that if I had been a German, acting as I did, in France I'd have been shot several times.*

"But at last I did get away properly. Got into Holland. But I was all broken up, as I am now. No, I haven't got a sou of pension. Yes, but, you know what it is, a thing like this is difficult to prove."

His doom, however, could not mitigate the sourness of the baker's blood. It was he who so violently urged that the guillotine should be used on the girl who killed her baby. It was, of course, inevitable that the contrast between his own position and that of Lemoule should arouse bitterness in him. So we heard the first version of Lemoule's career through the lips of an enemy:

* Maybe the baker magnified his dangerous qualities.

"That fellow, why, when war broke out he ran away to Spain. And Spain kicked him out as an undesirable. So he bunked off to America, where he cowered till America comes into the War and then he's got to go. Nowhere else to run away to. And then he got into some silly accident, not war at all, was pinched a bit, squealed; and now comes over here like a *sacré* millionaire. Pah!"

* *
*

The peasant family is a working organism, slackness it cannot, dare not tolerate. Before the advent of Lemoule the tobacconist-cooper's unit was complete. He had a tiny shop with about two square yards of small-paned window in which was displayed one chiffon hat of a past mode, one large doll dressed in infantile luxury, three picture postcards and a varnished painting of an ornate young woman to advertise sewing-cotton.

The aged mother, telescoped and quivering with age as though continuously a-shudder at the approach of death, sat behind a small counter and did her best with palsied hands to measure out snuff and tobacco and to juggle change. The daughter Yvonne cooked and—having been trained as a *modiste*—made unfashionable hats for the farmers' wives at an average of three or four per annum. The cooper-tobacconist did the rest. He felled trees, sawed planks, made barrels, dug, mowed, planted, gathered, pressed wine, etc., mutable as the seasons. Now, into this self-contained family is thrust a stranger, not only a stranger but one who protests that he is incapable of working. There can be little doubt that Lemoule's 700 francs a month outweighed by a large amount the other earnings of the combined family, and that his capture put it into a state of affluence hitherto undreamed of, that Lemoule with his money alone pulled more than his weight.

But the peasant family cannot get over its prejudice about work. Lemoule, after his newness had worn off, struck that family with a horror equal to what would be produced in a righteous Victorian family by a visit from Huxley. Lemoule was an agnostic to the religion of work. To add to his crime Lemoule appeared fit enough. A dropped foot is not a very palpable deterrent from work, and nervous weakness is a malady which has no place in the peasant pharmacopœia. So that in time the cooper—not one of the highest intelligences in Janac—came to look upon his son-in-law as a lazy, good-for-nothing, shirking house-cumberer. Yvonne, a very nice girl, was torn between two instincts, the love for her husband and the peasant tradition. She was irritated at him for " wasting his time."

Nor was Lemoule contented with his lot. He had lived for the greater part of his life in large cities or on ocean steamers. The cramped inquisitions of village existence, exacerbated as they were by the peculiar circumstances of his position, by his exorbitant pension, by his change of nationality and so on, annoyed and wounded him. The peasant satisfaction at its own slyness contrasted with its arrogant conservatism exasperated him. The hampered conditions of family agriculture and the meagre profits resulting from such village enterprises as tobacco-selling and hat-making disheartened him. For instance, the tobacco trade. The cooper's shop, the only one in the lower village, sold about sixty kilos of tobacco a month. The average profit was about one sou per packet of twenty grammes or fifty sous a kilo, so that profit on tobacco amounted to 150 francs a month. With the tobacco trade went stamps and matches, on which profits were minimal. Two hundred francs at the outside represented the labour and trouble of keeping the shop, from which must be deducted the expenses of two fortnightly journeys to Francheville including meals there, of the transport of the goods and of loss incurred by supplies of mouldy tobacco which the company—being a Government monopoly—refused to make good.

* * *

Lemoule was intelligent, and had a sense of humour, but one can only be intelligent and amused about a thing as long as one can stand away from it. Once in earnest it is almost impossible to remain either cool-minded or humorous, nobody is as intelligent about what *really* matters to him, for intelligence has that touch of godhead which makes the whole of man seem kin in futility. Here was a pretty setting for a tragedy of ordinary human nature. Lemoule was a part of it. He made his position worse by open criticisms, which of course irritated the villagers. Old habit and custom reserves to itself the right to criticize, it does not feel that *it* can give offence; but should the criticized retort, it becomes annoyed. We can, perhaps, illustrate the quality of Lemoule's intelligence by saying that his favourite authors were, in English, Jack London, in French, Octave Mirbeau. He liked Jack London because of the somewhat naïve philosophy he found in the books—through Jack London he could view life in a simplified formula; he liked Mirbeau because Mirbeau could hate, because Mirbeau hated snobbish shams, bourgeois cowardices, peasant insensibilities, and indeed everything which makes man—not lesser than the angels indeed, but lesser than man.

Lemoule could scent tragedy in the air about him and was struggling to escape from it. He knew that he must get away from the village; he must get his wife away from the village. The chance was opened to him haphazard fashion, as most things come in life. He had amateured with the violin, so little seriously indeed that his was still the three-quarter size instrument which his father had bought him when a lad. The schoolmaster of the *école laïque*, trying to make headway in the village against the theatrical displays of the Church school, organized a fortnightly cinematograph entertainment. He scrambled together an orchestra consisting of two violins, an accordion and a clarinet. Lemoule was the second violin. As he sat in the semi-gloom playing his not too complex part of the general noise, with a wandering eye taking in scenes of derring do, depicted from his position in startling perspective, he suddenly envisaged the means of escape. Could he but master his instrument well enough only to play a part in a serious cinematograph orchestra there was yet an object for him in life. He had heard vaguely of re-education bureaux in America, for damaged soldiers. Could he get one to help him, to a conservatoire or something?

He broke the news of the scheme, perhaps too abruptly to his relatives. His whole family were combined against him, even his wife. Each member had a positive personal reason to resent his departure. The old woman depended upon her granddaughter's help; the cooper saw 700 francs a month walking out of the house; the wife, whose sole experience out of the village had been a brief honeymoon at the house of Lemoule's father—at a retired villa in one of the more bric-à-brac suburbs of Paris—was terrified of having to plant new roots and of having to recommence existence, to make new friends.... Ah! Again, had Lemoule proposed any other means of life he might have been listened to, if he had wished to become carpenter or bricklayer or

house painter these were respectable trades, but musician, artist! The whole peasant conscience revolted at the idea. To the peasant there seems something immoral in the artist. Whenever life becomes really worth living, the artist at once takes a high and proper place in the community; he represents the fullness of life reaching out to grasp at something beyond the edge of normal apprehension. But as long as life is merely the stress and struggle of living—in a beleaguered city or on the raft of the Medusa, to quote extreme cases—there is no room for the artist, he is a cumbersome nuisance and his aspirations may be a definite evil. Civilization has ordained that the greater part of its producers shall live under such a stress and at least on the precarious edge of privation. So that, though these producers may in their moments of relaxation allow themselves to enjoy art, provided it be of a lethargic or sensuous nature, the contempt for the artist—the producer of *unnecessary* things—is ingrained: a contempt, indeed, so ingrained that it filters up even to those grades which *need* art; and it is almost always for some worldly reason that a living artist at last gains a condescending admiration.

The whole peasant family revolted at the idea, an artist, *un crève la faim*. Peuh! What would people say about them, a musician, a mountebank? Besides, didn't everybody know that Lemoule was no artist ? This art stuff is heaven-born, one doesn't *begin* to be an artist at thirty. Was not his cousin a more talented player ? Did *he* propose to become artist ? and so on, and so on. One can imagine the scenes in that grim stone house with its small windows and no damp courses, in those dimly lit, *pratique* interiors with beds contrived in the walls, under the staircases; hands waving, heads nodding, gesticulations, lost tempers, sulks, sneers, sharp answers. Seven hundred francs walking out of the house; worth a struggle to retain; an *artist* in the family to boot.

Madame Yvonne Lemoule was more than pretty. She was also impressionable, and it is a cause of jar in many families that women often allow themselves to be swayed more by old habit than by new love. The fear of experiment is a part of their social being. I don't think that Madame Lemoule viewed our coming with any gratitude. I think that Lemoule is the kind of man who escapes—had he not escaped from Paris even in his youth? But at the moment when we arrived he seemed to be conquered.

Circumstances had played against him. A woman lawyer in America, one who had helped him with his pension arrangements, had sounded the re-education bureau; but re-education was reserved for residents in America: America wasn't going to re-educate Lemoule for the benefit of France. Still, the lawyer saw hopes of making another effort, if he could find a good conservatoire in France. But his family made capital of the letter. After the disappointment Lemoule's badgered nerves gave way, he felt capable of struggling no longer. He was beaten for the moment.

For the moment he was beaten. With some pain to himself he helped the cooper get in the hay, he hoed between the potatoes, he drove the donkey down into the brushwood patch. He had the rather unsatisfactory pleasure of knowing that he, a grown man, was about as useful as a boy of twelve. For the moment he was beaten. But he would have escaped. He would probably have escaped in exasperation and tragedy —as the world counts tragedy. Madame Lemoule never realized that we will probably be her saviours. We came blatantly artists,—painters and musicians. We had no intention of helping Yvonne Lemoule, we only realized— gradually through a host of vague implications and half-effaced regrets—that an artist was here held in bondage by the Philistines. " An artist ? " you say. " Was Lemoule, then, an undiscovered genius ? " No, he had talent and what is as important—persistence—but was not a genius. However, Art does not consist in genius. Art is, in a way, any attempt to escape with self-respect from the practical life. Art is making unnecessary things or putting unnecessary qualities into necessary things. One of my favourite sayings is that in *Providence and a Guitar*—" Art is not water-colour sketches or playing on the piano. It is a life to be lived." Here was a putative artist—imprisoned.

Young Madame Yvonne resented our interference. They had got him so nicely locked in, he had tried his little file on one of the bars, and dismayed to see how tiny an effect was produced he had almost given up. We could but encourage him to file away, to try another bar, we could but describe the beauty of the freedom outside.

Madame Yvonne didn't know that we were fighting for her happiness ; that if Lemoule could escape now he would carry her with him to a new, a more expanded life. She didn't know that if they succeeded in holding him either one of two things would ensue : she would have gained an increasingly exasperated, increasingly irritated, increasingly objectionable partner, or she would one day awake to find him vanished, to find herself husbandless.

*_**

This is a story you may end your own way, for the end is not yet. Lemoule is still filing, though not one bar has ceded, the bars are thinner. He is still searching for a convenient conservatoire. He is at the practising for five or six hours a day; his touch is remarkably clear on the high notes and the sound of his violin makes his father-in-law grit his teeth with rage.

For ourselves we have little doubt that one day Lemoule and his wife will tap at our studio door in Paris, smilingly apologetic.

VIII

THE MOUNTAIN FIRES AROUND THE VILLAGE

VILLAGE life may be expected to provide less incident than material for reflection, for, indeed, is not the chief complaint against village life that it is dull? And here the casual guest may go very astray in his estimate of the interest of village existence, what may be incident for him is often mere sameness or commonplace for the villagers. Still, we must admit that the dullness of village life is due in some extent to an inherent human defect, that normal humanity has to *be* interested, it is unable to interest itself.

Yet we may be tempted to consider the mountain fires as incident, perhaps not altogether a desirable incident from the angle of village prosperity, yet a most decided breaking of monotony for the moment. The fires were afternoon and evening entertainments, entertainments or tragedies, which you will, though if you count them as tragedies they were tragedies of slackness, of jealousy, of disorganization, rather than tragedies of material loss.

The sun had flung its withering heat across the ridges of the Rouergue, and for several months no rain had fallen. The grass and undergrowth were yellow, and the heat haze made all the chestnut groves—which alternating with stubble cut the hills into a harlequin's coat of green and pallid gold—quiver as though all the trees were a-trembling at

MOUNTAIN FIRES AROUND THE VILLAGE

the drought. Janac had its three trains daily, with a certain rumbling passage of irregular goods waggons drawn by hoarse, out-of-date machines. But it always seemed to be the engine of the eleven o'clock express, a modern, high-boilered affair of great length, short funnel and complex machinery, which tossed sparks so lavishly into the dried grass and bracken of the cliff's edge.

It was on a Sunday morning while walking from the *remise* to the " hotel " that we perceived behind the massed groves of chestnut and walnut on the far side of the nearest valley a faint perpendicular stain on the sky—as though a piece of blue silk had been ineffectually cleaned after an accident with a tea-cup. We took but little notice of the effect. Here and there, more distantly, it had shown up before, we had more than once promised ourselves a catastrophe such as one encountered in Bosnia the year before, when several miles of forest were ablaze, but these stains of smoke had soon died down.

However, by the time that we had finished our daily chat with Monsieur Lemoule, we perceived from the gathering crowd at the edge of the parapet that this fire was arousing village interest. We joined the villagers to find that our wavering ribbon had woven itself into a broad, slowly rising translucent curtain which at its upper edge drifted away in thin clouds of wood smoke. The fire was hidden from us, on the far side of the hill, so that the edge of the chestnut groves stood sharply drawn against the smoke. But, even as we watched, the smoke took on a more intense tint, it thickened, it began to cumulate and to roll, while between the trunks of the farthest trees quivered a sharp orange glimmer. Now for a moment a scarf of flame was brandished in the air, and to our listening ears came a faint sound, as of a silk dress rustling. Beyond the crest of the chestnuts rose the ridge of a farther slope, apportioned out in vines, grass and brushwood, and on its extreme crest now a small grove of trees surrounding a farm-house. From where we stood we could see one or two figures, infinitely small, running to and fro across the grass and through the vines, with a semblance of distraction curiously resembling that of ants who have lost their way back to the nest. The villagers of Janac clustered more thickly at the edge of the parapet. They were stiff with the ceremony and the relaxation of Sunday.

"The Sestrols have vineyards on that far hill," said somebody eagerly, "so has the *garde champêtre*. Will the fires get as far? Besides, the *garde champêtre* has just stacked up a hundred faggots or so of brushwood. They'll burn nicely, eh?"

We took our sticks and set off for the top of the chestnut wood, half hoping to take part in some collective fire fighting. The road led us past the ox-dock—stout erection of square beams, roofed over with red tiles—past the Church schools, from which the wife of the schoolmaster (an ex-friar) with her baby and goat was now setting off for the old fortress, past the wheelwright's, along a glowing road on either side of which were hedges thick with the despised blackberry and with sloes, between vineyards where the last blue bloom of the copper sulphate sprayings was fading back to the green leaf. A country lane plunged us between steeply sloping hayfields, and a footpath lifted us steeply into the chestnut woods. We had made a long detour up to the head of a valley and back along the other side. Under our eyes Janac spread itself out along its curved ridge.

The chestnut wood was not broad here, and by hollow roads we walked through it out on to the hill-side beyond.

We now stood over an amphitheatre of hill-side, a majestic curve mottled with wood, with brush and with cultivation. At its foot the fire, almost invisible in the strong sunlight, was advancing slowly upwards and across, spreading as it came.

It was not a spectacular fire, for in that strong light both fire and smoke were almost invisible. There was little, but varying wind, so the destruction spread slowly and spasmodically, giving the appearance more as if some ink-blot, thrown down on to a yellow absorbent paper, were increasing gradually by capillary attraction. Slowly the blackness of ashes was substituted for the fawn and gold of the dry summer. The withered grass and brushwood gave themselves heartily to the flames, but the bigger trees had yet enough sap in them to resist in appearance, they stood like sturdy Quakers amid a frenzy of war. The fire ducked into the woods, crept through, swallowing the undergrowth, and emerged triumphantly upon the far side. Immediately below us the flames were coming nearer. In the thin smoke at the edge of a vine patch two women and a man were beating out the fire with green boughs. Now we could hear how when the fire made a dart into half-dried bushes it gave out a crackling roar, and beyond the silhouettes of the fire fighters we could see the ashes of burned grass and leaves whirled up into the stinging air.

A spectator joined us on the hill-side. He was a man heavy both for his years and for his height. He was dressed in grey flannels and on his head he wore a strange panama hat, with a small brim, like an upturned basin, encircled with a very gay ribbon, scarlet, green and black. In a few moments he had introduced himself.

"Jacques Degrain," he said, bowing, "collector of taxes."

"Jan Gordon," I returned with an answering salute, "painter of pictures, and Madame Gordon, painter also."

"It interested me greatly to hear that you were painters," said the tax-collector. "Indeed, I feel that I must charge myself with the painters who honour Janac. I am considered quite an authority on the beauty spots round about. I am pleased to take painters about in my car. Last year, for instance, I had the honour of conducting a gentleman who was painting farm-yards, exclusively farm-yards. Landscape? He snapped his fingers at it. He was, he told me, an expert at farm-yards, he had medals at the Salon, recompenses from every country in Europe. Oh, a great painter, but exclusively of farm-yards. I was able to find him several most satisfactory farm-yards. He kindly allowed me to watch him paint. I reveal myself, monsieur. I too am of the confraternity, an amateur only alas, a lover. But I sold a picture last year, in Toulouse, for thirty francs. It will greatly interest me to show you places in which to paint, and you will give me a criticism or two and allow me to gather hints from watching you at work."

To this kindly-made offer of the tax-collector we gave an answer which was not as grateful in thought as it was in word. The artist does, by his very profession, expose himself while at his artistic creation to the curiosity and the comment of the passer-by, but he rarely invites such curiosity or comment. Few persons would be hardy enough to propose to lean over the shoulder of and make comments to an author or a composer of music while at work ; so, why a painter should be supposed to be so much less susceptible we cannot imagine. Nor could we feel that the pleasure proposed—of dashing in a motor-car to sketch some view delectable to the tax-collector—was worth the price demanded. So we expressed ourselves in ambiguous terms on this point, nevertheless offering most enthusiastically to give him hints and to criticize his work. What human being can resist the office of mentor ?

We had meanwhile been sauntering through some long grass on the hill-side towards a point where the flames were making greater headway. In the far distance we could see a couple of figures energetic in a patch of vines, we deduced them to be Sestrol and Raymond waiting the approach of the fire to the edge of their vineyard. To the right, lower down the slope, the flames rushing up a dry gulley with the noise of an express train had surrounded the vineyard of the *garde champêtre* and were making a vivid bonfire of his stacked brushwood.

" Excuse me," said the tax-collector. " I think that we had better retreat from this spot. If the flames advanced by that hedge to the right and if they came up that piece of wood to our left, and if a gust of wind should spread them behind us, we would be surrounded. It is a very painful death."

As there was little wind, and as the flames in general were progressing at the speed of about one mile per hour, the risks of an impromptu *auto-da-fé* on that hill-side seemed very remote. However, we thought it best not to argue, and so retreated to some ploughed land where the tax-collector assured us we might remain with considerable safety.

" And yourselves," asked the tax-collector as soon as

all danger was past, " might I be bold and inquire what is your speciality in painting ? "

" Speciality ? " said we.

" Why, yes," replied the tax-collector. " Do you paint portraits or landscapes or nature-mortes, or genre pictures or battle pieces or religious subjects ? What, in fact, is your—well, speciality ? "

We answered that we painted anything which pleased or interested us.

" You—er—you do not specialize ? " asked the tax-collector.

" No," we answered stoutly ; " painting is painting."

The admiration in the tax-collector's eye dimmed into doubt. Could persons, he was wondering, who did not specialize, be *really* serious ?

Three hundred yards away a small isolated vineyard with a stone shed built upon it was now at the edge of the fire ; at this spot the flames were low, grass and small hill shrubbery providing the fuel, but owing to a fair amount of green stuff the smoke was thicker than is general. Through the intermittent curtain of flame could be seen a woman hard at work with a long bough beating the fire from the borders of her property. A small child, now seen, now lost in the smoke, was aiding her with great energy.

" Ah ! Ah ! " cried the tax-collector suddenly, with a sound of pain in his voice. " It is Maria, rash foolish woman. She has taken her child too. They will be killed, asphyxiated, burned up. Oh ! Oh ! It is so painful a death, so painful. How rash, how rash ! And she *was* such a good woman, so kind-hearted, so good-humoured. Oh, Maria, Maria, why were you so reckless ! Nothing can be done, they cannot be saved. They are surrounded. What a terrible death ! "

But Maria, in spite of her funeral oration, continued to beat the flames with vigour, while her small daughter ran to and fro enjoying the fun.

However, the anticipated fate of Maria did not long hold the tax-collector's attention, and he made no move to the rescue. He told us that he had a great admiration

THE FIRE IN THE BRUSH.

for the English, that at one time in his life he had read and spoken English with some fluency, but that he had forgotten everything. The study of English is, in fact, becoming very popular in France. Where formerly one found nobody with a word of our language, nowadays the lads and lasses from school speak with much better results than are produced by a corresponding study of French in England. We said something of this nature to the tax-collector, who was interested to hear it, and by gradual means we came to sport. Of late years, agreed the tax-collector, France had begun to take an interest in sport. However, he added, that after a serious test in the schools sport had been dropped as an important part of the youthful training system; it had been proved by experiment that sport and the concentration on sport had an atrophying effect on the intellect.* He said that France could not encourage the prospect of healthy dunces as a national ideal: France was the intellectual country of Europe *par excellence*, she must remain so.

We had been strolling back along the edge of the chestnut woods, through patches of vine planted in rows, mostly young plants recently grafted. Now we came to a field of potatoes on the lower edge of which two men were reclining in the shade smoking cigarettes.

"You are taking things easy," said the tax-collector to them.

"Well, monsieur, what will you?" answered one of them. "We came out to see if we could stop the fire from getting into the chestnut woods, but nobody comes to help us, and two alone are not sufficient. So there's nothing to do about it."

And the speaker gave a most expressive shrug. Resignation had so clearly claimed him that to offer a help would have been a mere foreign impertinence. The fire at this point, perhaps overmuch for two men, was not too violent for half a dozen. It was creeping forward through the grass and shrubs, against what little wind there was, and its

* "L'education publique ne résondra jamais le problem difficile du développment simultané du corps et de l'intelligence."—BALZAC.

progress was leisurely to a degree. The tax-collector stood looking at the fire for some time, then turning on his heel proposed that we should return home.

THEORETICAL PAINTING!

We may here remark that the tax-collector's threat to take us view-hunting came to nothing. He happened one day shortly afterwards to come upon Jo as she was beginning a sketch in oils. Her methods are experimental rather than conventional, and the poor tax-collector, used to the precise methods of the *specialist*, stared flabbergasted at an underpainting in primitive colours. At last he found words:

"You, you do theoretical painting then, madame," he gasped, and from that day avoided us, as much as was consistent with courtesy.

We said adieu to the tax-collector, and took another road homewards, descended into the valley by vague tracks through the chestnut wood, crossed the bed of the small stream which the drought had dried up, and clambered by paths through the terraced gardens of Janac till we arrived once more at the Hôtel Sestrol with its still-assembled crowds of Sunday spectators.

By this time the fire had got into the chestnut plantations. Its path of entry was no broader than half a dozen sporting workmen could have held in check; but we found a curious apathy concerning the fire. It was Sunday, people who were cleaned up and in fresh linen were not going out to soil themselves with fire. Then, the place of entry was on the land of a Monsieur Aubiel, and Monsieur Aubiel was not resident in Janac. One could not disturb one's self for the woods of Monsieur Aubiel: perhaps one was not so sorry that Monsieur Aubiel's woods were burning. From the woods of Monsieur Aubiel the fire spread into those of Monsieur Porphy, the father of Mlle. Cécile. Mlle. Cécile was herself at first childishly delighted. "No chestnuts to pick up this year, thank heavens!" she exclaimed, clapping her hands. Later, she came back shaking her head with that French look of brooding seriousness and of omniscient wisdom. "But it is serious, very, very serious. Father says we shall lose a lot of money."

We were surprised to note the general apathy of the

villagers to the fires. The chestnut groves are considered to be the chief source of Janac's wealth. The chestnuts, a very fine variety, are almost all exported to England, and many of the villagers gain large sums yearly in the speculation; for speculation it is. The villager gathers the fruit, or brings it in sufficient quantities to fill a railway truck, sends it off carriage paid to Covent Garden, and must wait often for months to find out for what his chestnuts have sold.

There seemed to be in this village of landowners, in this village of self-government, in this village of democracy, not the faintest stirrings of communal spirit, none of that clannishness which would have sent a whole English or American village rushing to the aid of one of its members. Janac's wealth was burning, *eh bien!* it was not the wealth of Janac, it was the wealth of Monsieur Aubiel, of Monsieur Porphy. Yet Monsieur Porphy came out with his wife to shake his head despondently over his consuming woods, but took no measures to save them. For a couple of hundred francs he could have fought the fire from his boundaries. He made no move. The fire was in the undergrowth, the chestnut trees themselves seemed to be resisting the flames, except where here and there some older tree with a hollow stem offering extra hold to the flames sprang up in a column of fire, becoming more lurid as the light was fading. But in the undergrowth the fire was burning steadily, charring the tree trunks, so that the trees which seemed so steadily to resist the fire were in a week great golden masses of a premature autumn and decay. Monsieur Porphy only shook his head.

"Those trees," he said, "will all be ruined, ruined. And think how many years will be needed to grow new ones in their place."

No, Monsieur Porphy would not save his trees because he could not have got Monsieur " Chestnuts," his next neighbour in the wood, to help. He would not expend his money alone in order to save Monsieur " Chestnuts " ; while Monsieur " Chestnuts " would not contribute to save Monsieur Porphy : why, the fire might never reach Monsieur " Chestnuts' " woods at all, travelling against the wind as it was. There was, in fact, a lack of cohesion, a want of sense of the general good, exemplified again in the matter of the post-office, of which we will treat later.

The fire progressed steadily through Monsieur Porphy's woods, and in an hour's time Monsieur " Chestnuts " was running to and fro in an agitated manner, wringing his hands, nodding his head and exclaiming :

" But it is very serious, very, very serious. In a few moments *my* wood will be on fire."

We call him " Chestnuts " because we do not know his name. He had introduced himself to us early in our stay by inquiring the present price of chestnuts in England, a piece of information we were unable to give. He had talked chestnut speculation with some seriousness and so had earned his sobriquet. He had a fine old house next to the Mairie, with a huge, square, beamed kitchen filled with old copper and pewter. He was reputed rich as Crœsus, dressed always like a labourer, did all his carting personally, and was, we suspect, the chief promoter of the gossip that we were spies.

By the time we went to supper the dusk had fallen and the hill-side presented a curious picture, the dark mass of the hill cut by a sinuous frontier of flame, while in the conquered territory only here and there a still smouldering or flickering tree spotted the blackness of the night. Later we went out to the fortress and gazed down the valley of

JANAC FROM THE HILLSIDE

the Aveyron. The flames still burning steadily were now some miles down the valley and drew an immense flourish of flame athwart the distant hills.

Luckily for Monsieur " Chestnuts " the thinning of the undergrowth extinguished the fire, which was advancing towards his woods. On the next day he was all smiles and complacency. But the fire still progressed downhill and the *garde champêtre* was stationed at the edge of the gulley to give instant warning should the fire cross the river-bed.

Janac went to bed in trepidation. Every one was murmuring that there was a terrible danger of a change in the wind. Then the flames would drive across the brook, up the terraces, and Janac would be a prey to the flames. If the fire should gain the village it would be serious enough. Every house with its attics stuffed with straw, hay and brushwood was a promising bonfire. There was a shortage of water as the village council, in spite of having ample funds, would not enlarge the reservoir; already we were on water rations, the fountains being closed at 6 p.m. and opened at 7 a.m.

We went to bed reflecting that six men on the borders of Monsieur Aubiel's territory would have saved all this loss, all this present anxiety.

* * *

The juxtaposition of feeble communal sense (team work) with keen republicanism tempts one to make a very tentative deduction. We must first of all assert that republican feeling was strong in Janac. There is a growing royalist movement in France—or at all events a movement which if not growing in numbers is increasing in noisiness—and Janac thought fit upon the 14th of July to celebrate its disapprobation by a dinner of patriots. Royalism was publicly condemned.

It is, I think, popularly considered that republicanism or democracy is a step towards communism, that it is the point where autocracy or the authority of one begins to fade into communism or the equality of all. But we venture to suggest that this is by no means the case, and that republicanism stands at one end of the line opposed to both autocracy and to communism at the other end. Republicanism is an

THE OLD PIGEON LOFT.

individualistic method of ruling, it is most successful when each man has a positive belief that *his* good is the good of the State, in which he sends *his* deputy up to represent him, to represent his village, his department: its decisions are drawn up by conflict, to which the person less powerful has agreed peacefully to submit. In republicanism the ruler is permitted to rule so long as he satisfies the mob. But communism—in which all the members of a community are organized to one end, the common not the individual good—cannot exist as conflict, it can only exist by the existence of a definite aim to which the community is working. But poor humanity is only capable of finding a definite aim by two methods, (1) under pressure of immediate external danger; (2) under domination of a superior mental or physical force. Communism must be the result of some external tyranny. So that communism seems possible only (1) spasmodically or (2) under an autocracy. The proof being that the Russian attempt at communism could only take place under the autocracy of Lenin. In America we seem to see a curious state of affairs. In spite of the professed hate of communism in America, the Americans with their social restrictions, compulsory temperance, etc., are attempting to graft some of the effects of communism on to a basis of republicanism. The individualistic reaction against the experiment is growing in force daily.

**

By the next morning the fires had died down, leaving some three or four square miles of burned territory to the south of Janac. The vineyards alone remained green and blooming on a landscape drawn literally in charcoal. The owners had, as a rule, given themselves some pains to preserve their grapes, but might have saved themselves the trouble, for the plants were green, the soil tilled, and there was no danger of harm other than the scorching of a few outer leaves. Indeed, the *garde champêtre* had left his vineyard to chance and it had suffered no more than had the others, though in a more exposed spot. Had those who worked so hard at the vines but mustered themselves along the edge of the chestnuts the woods would have been preserved. But that does not come within the republican creed.

THE MOUNTAIN FIRES

A week later a new fire broke out on the hill to the north of Janac. The hill was exclusive shrubbery and small trees, and burned with a much more exciting spectacularity than had the Southern slopes.

Raymond Sestrol was in particular distress. He had only the year before bought a wood on this very hill. Would the flames reach Raymond's wood ? Alas ! *Quel malheur!* Raymond's wood was attained, it was consumed. Madame Sestrol was distressed almost to tears. "*Le pauvre* Raymond," she exclaimed, " and he only bought it last year, how unfortunate."

After consolations had been offered we demanded the value of the loss, and were surprised to learn that he had bought the whole piece—land, trees, fences and all—for the sum of about ten shillings. As the land remained, we must leave the reader to calculate the loss in material.

The fire burned with great persistence during the afternoon and in the early night, once more Janac went to bed in trepidation. On the next morning the fire had died down, but about ten o'clock it revived and spread with some decision in the direction of a fairly important house near the station. A demand was at once sent up for the fire-engine.

The chief fireman, the *garde champêtre*, was absent ; but his second in command, Raymond Sestrol, having the keys, the station was unlocked and the engine dragged out. It consisted of a barrel on wheels with a force pump and a few lengths of hose. A horse was needed, but the time was unpropitious, all available steeds were out at work, so ourselves and Lemoule proffering assistance, we, *i.e.* Lemoule, Raymond, the messenger from the chateau and ourselves, rolled the machine through the cobbled streets until we got it upon a steep high road down to the station, upon which road we had little to do other than steering the machine aright and checking its gravitational energy. We galloped downhill behind the enthusiastic fire-engine, which seemed all eagerness to get to work. The day was boiling hot, and before we had traversed half of the interminable slope of Janac we were asking ourselves if the joke were worth the sweating. We have, however—especially Jo has—a fortunate British pertinacity.

THE FIRE-ENGINE.

Crossing the bridge over the Aveyron we at last reached the château where willing assistance urged the fire-engine up a steep and difficult track until it emerged upon the hill fronting the thin line of advancing flame. There was not a drop of water nearer than the gardens of the threatened house, and so with a few buckets we began to fetch water which we poured into the engine. Raymond and my wife then seized the handles and, Lemoule guiding the nozzle, a meagre stream of water was directed upon the flames. After ten minutes of this work, however, it occurred to us that the simpler method of transferring the water directly on to the fire from the bucket was less fatiguing, less complicated, and more economical, since the hose leaked abominably. So with reluctance the fire-engine was abandoned, for the magic rather than the efficiency of the machine was what had been demanded, and the fires threatening the château were extinguished with great ease and rapidity.

Pleased with the success of our assistance we all went to drink a glass of wine at the café near the station and from thence returned home, leaving the fire-engine to be brought back at the convenience of the château cattle.

IX

FOUR DAYS OF VILLAGE FESTIVAL

PERHAPS the most striking distinction between the English and the French village lies in the total absence of what one may call gentle control. No squire's family here exercises its enlivening interest, the parson is himself a villager whose interference is more often repudiated than sought for, no glimmer of patronage hints to the villagers how the higher folk amuse themselves. When the village is *en fête* it is a village festival.

Every village has its yearly fête of more or less importance. Even Janac station, which boasts but three or four houses, held its yearly celebration and borrowed Janac's *château fort* for an effective though inexpensive illumination. Martinolles, the nearest railway station, also had its fête to which I went in Raymond's company, Jo with a headache remaining in Janac. She did not miss much of interest. Cou-Cou, the baker's assistant, is an indefatigable fête goer. To any fête within the reasonable distance of six miles he goes, dances all the afternoon in the sawdust, stays till the last Togne at night is equivalent to " auld lang syne," tramps home on tired feet and trusts to luck that he is back early enough to get the first batch of loaves—shaped like a penny bun but weighing two pounds—into the oven in time for the regular morning customers. Whenever he overstays his time the baker, choleric consumptive that he is, barks and coughs an indignant dismissal. Cou-Cou

 accepts his fate with resignation; goes to Francheville, gets the offer of a new job in no time, returns triumphantly to Janac where he is at once begged to stay, the baker having become afraid of the shortage of labour, knowing that if Cou-Cou goes he will be months without a man. Cou-Cou puts up with the baker's vagaries, for he has tender relations in Janac; he would in reality be loath to quit, there is a girl in the faubourg. . . .

Janac, like Gaul, is divided into three parts, for all that it is but a necklace swung on one long string of a street. There is the faubourg, snobbish upper village clustered about the Place de Grifoules with its aristocracy, the genial chemist, the mayor, the tax-collector, the bailiff and one doctor; there is the lower village, our village, with its aristocracy, Monsieur Porphy, Monsieur "Chestnuts," Dr. Saggebou, the *avocat* and the electrician (the Sestrols fall below the aristocratic); there is the old village clustering beneath the *château fort*, steep street of mediæval houses falling into ruin, mostly untenanted, with no aristocracy whatever. For most purposes, however, Janac is but twainly split, the faubourg and the lower village, and this unfortunate division is most noticeable at the fête. Janac fête lasts three days, or if the money collected is sufficient to tempt the orchestra, for four days. We sing, we dance, we parade the streets, we drink, we loaf for four whole days, days carefully set between the corn harvest and the grape gathering, so that no village occupation is greatly harmed by the holiday. During this time we of the lower village are in marked division with those of the faubourg; we are in rivalry with our *gâteaux*; our processions contest both in daily parade and in nightly illumination; we cannot meet without jeers of derision. A decade ago they used to come to active battle, during the fête the upper and lower villages broke one another's crowns with good will and solaced bruises with good wine. This year we had an unfortunate difference about a cornet player.

A good *piston*, as he is called, is naturally the backbone of an out-of-door band, and we counted ourselves fortunate in having engaged the services of an excellent player, but at the last moment, the perfidious faubourg having tempted him with promises of better pay, he left us in the lurch. Our *comité* was distracted, but at last, by representing the perfidiousness of the faubourg, the terrible predicament thus thrust upon it, by showing that the pride, the very honour of the lower village was at stake, the newsvendor was persuaded to take the place of the traitor. Now, the newsvendor had been first cornet in a Zouave regiment. He consented with reluctance, only a sense of wounded honour would have made him act, for he had also a café adjoining the market hangar in which the lower village danced, and he suspected the powers of his wife to gain the full benefit of the opportunity. The lower village sighed with relief, it even giggled with pleasure, for the ex-Zouave *piston* was locally renowned, the faubourg had put its own nose out of joint. But the faubourg got back at us in the affair of the big drum.

Janac fête is marked by one peculiarity, by its buns. The two days previous to the fête the whole village is flustered, cake-making, while the *comité* and its female aids themselves also labour over cakes for the fête itself: flour, eggs, sugar and milk go whirling round in the biggest copper cauldrons available, the great buns are moulded into the shape of the letter O, four feet in length, three feet across, and are thrust into a special oven in the bakehouse of the faubourg, while Cou-Cou is besieged by a crowd of women, each one begging precedence for her private cake in the smaller oven of the consumptive baker. Foremost comes the wife of the *garde champêtre*, hair wild, eyes staring, clamouring precedence for a wretched little lump of dough scarce worthy of the name "*galette.*" Then, when morning comes, what a flurry and an outcry : this one is done too much ; that one too little ; this one is baked on one side ; another woman is not contented, believing that the cake she receives back is not the one she deposited. The baker's wife, to make the sides more fair, woman against woman, comes volubly to the rescue of Cou-Cou ; the crowds diminish, and, last of all, palsied by wild fury, goes the wife of the *garde champêtre* carrying her little bun which had sadly shrivelled.

Ducks and chickens are hurried into their respective *basses-cours*, or hen-houses, where they remain prisoners for four days, their normal playground being the streets from which the noise of the bands would scatter them for the benefit of strangers. The two children of the private gentleman from Toulouse wander about with depressed faces, their peasant maternal grandfather, the ne'er-do-well, being seriously ill ; indeed, his son-in-law has been heard to express the hope that "the old fellow won't die during the fête and spoil the children's fun " ; the aristocratic shoemaker's fat wife is waddling about radiating beauty airs, the consumptive baker drags his deck-chair into the shadow of the Hôtel Sestrol and with cap tilted forward over his hollow eyes watches Monsieur Aristide Diadème superintending the decorations for the hangar, beneath which we are going to dance.

Monsieur Diadème is a typical village *fainéant*, being an artist who has lost his way in life. He has not quite the face of an artist, the successful painter as a rule tending to fatness. No, he has a lean and hollow look, which in Art usually denotes a second-rate talent; for instance, shave Horace Vernet, the battle painter, give him a drooping, almost Chinese  moustache and you have Monsieur Diadème. I fear, too, that the drooping moustache is a sign of failure. I can remember no genius except, perhaps, Robert Louis Stevenson who allowed his moustache to trail to his chin. His history is interesting and in some ways peculiar. "*Fainéant*," Madame Sestrol, who gave us the details, called him. "As a lad he would do no proper work, loafed in the fields, played silly musical instruments all his spare time, and finally absconded to a big town. There he took to playing a clarinet in the streets for a living (and probably not so bad a living either) until some personage, struck by his talent and his youth, offered him a job on the railway." (The logical connection is not clear, but the facts are attested.) At the railway Diadème showed himself *fainéant* as usual, until a presidential visit threw the place into a fluster of decoration, at which Aristide showed so much energy, ingenuity and taste that his career was henceforth settled, he became decorator for the stations of the P.L.M. He lived in a world of intermittent official rejoicing: if Lyons welcomed Monsieur Clemenceau it did so in the tinted raptures of Aristide Diadème, Marseilles did honour to Monsieur Poincaré in a like manner. No official visit was successful without his adornments, and during the quieter times of the political world he cut out flags, sewed bunting, designed streamers, constructed lanterns.

Now he has retired on a well-earned pension, but his habits are too strong for him. He has a donkey and cart, the cart is painted this month green and pink, last month it was blue and yellow, the donkey wears the most unusual head-dress of a white lambskin wig and looks extraordinarily like one of our more solemn barristers about to make a speech. His whip has a royal blue shaft. The colour of his wheelbarrow varies as often as does that of his cart, and as it is decorated with bells, Monsieur Diadème's grandsons count it a game to work for him, labour becomes a lark. At present his official position is art editor to the fête of the *lower* village of Janac.

Madame Sestrol has been busy making force-meat all the morning, the restaurant is full. The waitress who looks so like the mannequin is hard at work. She is waitress only on especial occasions, market days or times like these of fêtes: on ordinary occasions she is the village commissionaire, going to Francheville twice weekly for things which cannot be purchased in Janac. Her history is sad. Lively, energetic and bustling as she was, fate with its queer inconsequences sought her out for unhappiness. She was well dowered, and married to one of the most promising tradesmen in the village, the baker. He, however, went to the bad; drink and gambling did away with her fortune, misery and blows for herself and her child drove her distracted, till at last she had to be taken to the asylum. She came out five years later to find herself a widow with nothing left

PLACE DU GRIFOULES

but the bakehouse as property and her boy as comfort. So she has rented the bakery till her son is old enough to succeed to the business, and in the meantime she supports herself and him as best she can.

After lunch Monsieur Diadème is still putting last touches to the decorations of the hangar. The bandstand is a precarious-looking balcony slung by chains eight feet from the ground against the wall; on the other three sides the hangar is open. The beams are twisted with garlands of greenery, Japanese lanterns in profusion will give a romantic light; while two large box-like constructions of coloured glass and wood, decorated with a screed, "The gift of Citizen Diadème," provide a variety in lighting. The hard and flinty road, which is the floor of the hangar, is bedded under deep sawdust.

The afternoon draws on. The blacksmith to the left and the newsvendor to the right have mustered all the tables that they can on either side of the road, in the near distance Sestrol's hotel blossoms with all its fête-time temptations, hats, overalls, lively striped sponge cloths and the mannequin.

It is well three o'clock before the newsvendor, fattish and smiling, appears with his *cornet à piston* tucked under his arm, before other members of the band—a lanky clarionet, a robust euphonium and a side-drummer—begin to cluster in our little *place*. A sound of music from the Place de

Grifoules gives warning that the faubourg is moving, but we let it move: he laughs longest who laughs last. We are still slowly coagulating, with no evidence of purpose, when the procession from the faubourg surges down the narrow, steep street. Foremost comes the bun. It is a huge affair, bedecked with encircling ribbons of every hue. Lashed to three tall poles, it is carried, like some gigantic emblem, perpendicularly by three strong men, who stagger precariously under the weight in the uneven street. The band follows, our raped *piston* blowing unashamed in the lead. We scream derision. The procession lads and lasses of the faubourg, young and old footing it with *espadrilles* over the cobbles, swing past us, waving toy flags, returning abuse for abuse. They march through our *place*, plunge once again into the mediæval street which soars upwards again towards the *château fort*.

Now, hurry! Before they come back we must be in the faubourg. Diadème has a surprise for us. His donkey is led out resplendent in all the bells of the wheelbarrow and its judge's wig. Diadème himself appears dressed in old French costume, short jacket, striped trousers, cap of liberty; Cou-Cou comes travestied as a swashbuckler of Louis XV, woman's hat and feather, football jersey, knickerbockers, and a girl's cloak. Our bun, beribboned, topped by a brilliant silver star, is lashed to some sort of donkey furniture. Hurriedly it is fixed to Diadème's moke, two little platforms are provided for children, and Diadème's grandson and another are steadied aloft bearing a small tricolour apiece. Ha! That will surprise the faubourg.

But our innovations are not yet complete. Here comes the blacksmith, mounted on Bijou, Potato's horse, with large crossed flags at the front of the saddle. Bijou is a ponderous animal, steady as a rule, but liable to stumble, for its hoofs are too large and it trips up over itself if it is urged too fast: so Potato bought it cheap, Potato's business

THE PROCESSION.

not being of a pressing order. To-day, however, the waving flags startle Bijou just as the blacksmith is taking the head of the procession. It flings up its heels and the blacksmith is ignominiously capsized.

Off we go, up into the Place de Foultres, where the strange houses seem to peer at us like spectators leaning forward their chins on their arms and their elbows on their knees. Ta-ra-ta-ra-ta-ra, it's easier to play going up hill than down, not so much chance of a stumble, besides, our ex-Zouave can play that miserable traitor all round the town. Surely the faubourg are green with envy. The Place de Foultres, compared to the rest of Janac, is like a square buckle at the end of a long narrow strap, up one side we go, across the top—ta-ra-ta-ra, under the walls of the old hotel-keeper who cut off his nose to spite his face in the matter of the post-office, down the other side, back again into the narrow street, across the triangular *place*, into the narrow street once more—here we meet the faubourg procession coming back, yells, catcalls, orchestral opposition: *Viva le Joya, fidon la tristessa*—on, on, past the old granite fountain, past Dr. Saggebou's, past the electrican's—the drought is so bad we are forced to light this year's fête with candles—along the narrow streets once more, here's Lawyer Double-comb's, here's the convent, here's the Church girls' school. In a little open space, the castle reaching high on its peak to peer over the house roofs at us, we turn and take our homeward path. The musicians are out of breath, only the drum-taps still guide our unanimous steps.

Back the way we came, back to the triangular *place*, across it diagonally, past the Hôtel Sestrol, past Potato's, past the mad priest's, past the aristocrat shoemaker's, past the blacksmith's, to the hangar, to our dance hall. Here, while the blacksmith cautiously dismounts from Bijou, we form a farandole and caper in swaying lines of mingled youth and age, laughter and screams, about Diadème's donkey and our monstrous bun.

**

After supper Janac fête enters on its second phase, a phase of some beauty, in which we of the lower village were undoubtedly beaten by the faubourg, after having wrested from them the palm during the afternoon. Concerning the afternoon's performance, by the by, the faubourg was angered, it clamoured that we had outraged precedent. From times immemorial the *galette*—so they claim—has been borne aloft by the strong arms of men, in substituting the ass carrier and the children rampant as supporters we have broken with the past. The faubourg is academically outraged; how often must one preach to the *passéists* that a custom is only vital as long as it is living, as long as it is capable of change ? how often must one repeat that the rigid is dead ? A fig for your academics, who wants to *preserve* old customs ? The problem is to keep them living. When they die, let them go ; mummies are better in museums than capering puppet-wise in the open air.

Darkness had fallen on Janac streets before we had finished our cabbage *farci*, our roast duck, our Cammembert and *cantaloup*, before we had come to the coffee which this night we dared, fearing no one-o'clock vigil on the pillow. In the gloom of one electric street-lamp, ill supplied with current, the cortège was forming. The *galette* reposed peacefully somewhere in shelter, " *Cortège aux flambeaux* " this was called on the posters which Janac had distributed to all the surrounding villages. Flambeaux it should have been, resinous torches would indeed have made the past live again, but innovation is not without its beauty. Japanese

182 FOUR DAYS OF VILLAGE FESTIVAL

women had worked that Janac streets should this evening blush rose and green: "*Cortège aux lanternes japonaises*" should have been the script. Strange that the East should thus flaunt luminously through these streets which existed before the East had appeared into the knowledge of Europe.

MONSIEUR DIADÈME'S PLAN.

Three or four frames of light wood carried lanterns set in pattern, then came the band, after which followed the populace carrying lanterns in their hands. But the faubourg standards of swinging globes of paper were better designed than were ours, there were more, and each contrasted pleasantly in pattern with that which went before, ours were,

FOUR DAYS OF VILLAGE FESTIVAL 183

we must confess, higgledy-piggledy in effect. Monsieur Diadème had had no experience in "*Cortège aux flambeaux*"—official receptions do not reach such heights of gratification.

But deepest wound of all to our pride, the faubourg had abstracted the big drum. Thump, thump it went triumphantly, the sticks wielded by the smiling plump young man who on the day before had been introduced to Mlle. Cécile as prospective fiancé, on approval. For the moment they were sundered, he thumping the big drum for the faubourg, she swinging a lantern for the lower village, but after one night of enchanted dreams she was already blooming from an ordinary village maiden into a "*petite chatte amoureuse.*"

Spectators see most of the game, we exercised our privilege as visitors. We chose to watch, and the spectacle of those swinging processions in the strange old streets was both strange and fair, the faubourg got excited and soon were dancing in sinuous lines within the confined limits of their path, the standards of glowing globes tossed, and the train of lanterns swing to and fro, from time to time somebody lit a green or a red bengal light, which for a while extinguished all the lanterns in its more vivid glare. Then darkness snapped down again and the lanterns reappeared.

The same route was taken, but when the hangar was reached the lanterns were hung up, others were lit and the dancing began. It was not spectacular dancing; polkas, schottisches, waltzes and *pas de quatre* have ousted the old country-dances, the one step has appeared, but the tango and the shimmy have yet to reach Janac. Still, it was a good-humoured and a jolly whirl. Dancing in sawdust is a curious experience at first, but when one is accustomed to it the device works very well, and a good layer of sawdust makes quite a passable dancing-floor on a flinty road. The girls all lined up along the two sides of the hangar, and an especially beautiful effect was produced on the open side by the lines of flushed and excited faces glowing in the soft radiance of the Japanese lanterns contrasted with the lapis lazuli of a perfect Provençal night. The men, who usually deserted their partners immediately the dance was over, either ran into the cafés to get a drink or remained in groups, giggling surreptitiously, upon the road at either end of the hangar.

The aristocracy had taken tables either at the blacksmith's or at the newsvendor's, whence they amiably contemplated, occasionally taking part in, the gambols of their fellow villagers.

After a while we left *our* table at the newsvendor's and sauntered up to view the faubourg *en fête*. A portion of the green before the chemist's house had been made into a dance hall. Here was Arcady indeed. The space was enclosed with fresh-cut green boughs and saplings bodily planted, the sky made a roof and chains of coloured paper the cornices. The bandstand was a bower of green and the full moon hung over all, giving more light than the Japanese lanterns.

But the delightful dancing-place of the faubourg had one serious drawback in the eyes of frolicking youth, no café or drinking-house was near; woman there was, and music charmed, though with brazen rather than silver tongue, but wine, usually placed first in the trinity of bucolic happiness, was to seek. You had to go to the Place de Grifoules to get artificial excitement.

We went back to our own place, for long ago we had identified ourselves with the lower village. We found a table at the blacksmith's and continued to watch, occasionally joining in the dancing. After a while somebody was clamouring for a bourrée. The bourrée is the old customary dance of the country, how old we have not inquired, but John Sebastian Bach wrote bourrées for his Northern clientele. It was with some difficulty that four couples could be found to execute the dance, and three of the performers were grandparents. There is, we confess, in these old country-dances a kind of expansive gaiety which is most heartening, they are, so to speak, collective dances, the dancer must include his company, he is only an eighth of a dance. While these modern dances, these round dances, as one used to call them, are a limited individualistic kind of a pleasure, man and woman together being, I add, the most individualistic kind of individual possible. The truth is the world is becoming lazier, and individualism of this kind is the first foundation of laziness.

The night went on. After the bourrée, there was more good-humoured skipping. How different this mawkish whirling from the real grace necessary to make the bourrée a success! One by one the candles died out in the lanterns, slowly the night shadows crept in under the hangar from without.

At last the band decided that their money had been earned for the day, they yearned for bed and they yearned more effectively than the lads and lasses yearned for more dancing, they had the all-conquering yearn; and so the finale, *La Togne*, was decided upon. The music struck up very slowly and solemnly.

186 FOUR DAYS OF VILLAGE FESTIVAL

While the dancers gathered in long lines holding hands as if for a farandole. Suddenly the band turned into a brisk air:

and with the brisker music the linked dancers began to move in a swaying endless chain. Faster went the music,

LA TOGNE.

faster swung the dancers. In the once gay lanterns overhead the candles had by now almost all guttered down to a flickering extinction, only one or two survived, throwing a light on to the forms of the dancers, a light all the more diminished because on the road beyond the shadow of the hangar shone the vivid moonlight against which the dancing figures were silhouettes relieved with the faintest blushes of coloured light.

With an abrupt unexpectedness the band suddenly returned to the solemn, weird little air once more. At once the scene changed. The lines of frolicking dancers crouched suddenly down—with shrieks from the young women naturally—while over their heads into the circles leapt a lanky man brandishing a besom which he swung to and fro with a will. Anyone of the dancers standing erect received a clout on the head with the besom, a form of punishment often severe enough when the players were excited. Simple rustic game though it might be, the sight was almost strange, as can be imagined, the crouching, dimly-lit figures, the black wielder of the broom leaping from side to side recklessly over the lines of the dancers when hardy players in the distance tempted him to blows, the shrieks of the women, the moaning monotonous music : all this taking place in the dusky shadows of the hangar outlined only against the livid moonlight outside : Gagool's witch-finding in *King Solomon's Mines* could hardly have been a more uncanny spectacle. Indeed, it is more than probable that *La Togne* is a survival in dance of old village witch-huntings or of travestied Walpurgis nights.

The last candle flared out, the music ceased, *La Togne* was over, Janac went reluctantly to bed.

On every hand we were assured that Janac fête this year was of a diminished brilliance. The shortage of water in the river had so reduced the electric power that the lamps could hardly give enough light by which to read, and the fête was deprived of its purchased strings of electric globes of varied tints. Then, the drought and the consequent danger of fire had prohibited the enjoyment of fire-crackers, toy bombs and other explosive amusements with which youth harries age, a prohibition which, for us, detracted little from the enjoyment; but, as we have said before, the Latin adores noise. A certain amount of sore throat, however, was produced by the confetti, stamped out of paper often coloured with poisonous dye. This throwing of confetti shocked the peasant soul of Madame Sestrol. "It is scandalous," she said to us, "they are throwing *money* away." In the third place, Janac was suffering from competition. Long, long ago, Janac was a seneschal's residence, but slowly it is sinking to be an out-of-the-way anachronism. Far from lacking amusement, the country-side here, at this season, abounds in fêtes; every village, every hamlet has imitated the larger country centres; so that Cou-Cou could get himself an average of at least one fête a week, and the sack once a month. For instance alone, the village of St. Juery, on the far side of Albi, has a fête once every fortnight. Of course the village fêtes were simpler affairs than this of Janac, so needed less expenditure and were able to rival in attraction their more ambitious competitor, in consequence of which, as with the market, Janac fête, becoming but one amongst many, is losing value and importance.

On the second morning of the fête the orchestra, accompanied by two fête officials with red sashes, set out on the *quête*, the search for funds. In front of each house a short tune was played, a musical stand and deliver, to which the occupants could make no refusal. We, the casual visitors, and the unpropertied attendants at the fête, had paid our premium on the day before, collected on flag-day methods, receipted with a little rosette; we sported a green for the faubourg and a pink one from the lower village.

The afternoon of the fête repeated the performance of yesterday, only the blacksmith did not again tempt Providence on the back of Bijou, and after having led the bun back to the hangar we devoured it. Long tables were set under the roof, Monsieur Diadème with some ceremony divided the huge and, it must be confessed, stale *galette*.

PLAYING FOR FUNDS.

It was served to all comers with champagne and white wine. In the evening the dancing repeated that of the yesterday and was finished with *La Togne* in which Raymond received a black eye.

On the third day the processions were discontinued, we danced only, but in the evening a serious matter faced the partisans of the lower village. Money was short, it seemed

190 FOUR DAYS OF VILLAGE FESTIVAL

impossible to prolong the dancing till the fourth day, but the faubourg, richer than we, were making a four days' rejoicing of it. Could the lower village be disgraced by knuckling under to the faubourg ? A thousand times, no ! A second appeal to the patriotism of the lower village combined with a generosity on the part of the band—which consented to take lower fees for a final night—saved the honour of the lower village. A final *Togne* of unexampled weirdness and wildness, a *Togne* which persisted till all—dancers, witch-hunters and band—were exhausted, brought Janac fête to a successful conclusion.

Cou-Cou had taken the four days of Janac fête so enthusiastically that he was hardly fit to look at for four days after it.

X

THE ANCIENT CHURCH AND ITS LATTER-DAY PATRONS

JANAC church is a thirteenth-century building, an expiation for heresy. This village is on the northernmost fringe of that country infected by the strange beliefs of the Albigeois or Cathares. In these lands were practised the first inquisitions, predecessors to that Spanish Institution which has gained so great a notoriety; Fra Angelico, even, considered the Albigeois important enough for his paint-brush, and Simon de Montfort hoped upon the debris of their recantation to found a new royalty in opposition to that of France.

In broad outlines the Albigeois held that God was perfect and that, as from a good tree no evil fruit could come, perfection could not engender imperfection; that this imperfect earth therefore was the creation of an evil god. This evil spirit was named Lucifer, having a lieutenant named Lucibel and two female colleagues, Collant and Collibant. Men, however, they said, were angels seduced from heaven by the machinations of the evil spirits. They believed that man's sole aim was to regain his heavenly status; this he could do by a perfect life. Now, in heaven there is no marrying nor giving in marriage, so that the act of procreation is blatantly a device of the evil god. Moreover, all things produced by procreation are stained with this evil. Therefore the Albigeois believed that *all* procreation was evil, and that to consume flesh was to swallow evil matter: fish, not being propagated *in coitu impuro*, was, however, permitted. They were forbidden to kill anything except reptiles, which enclosed the spirits of Lucifer; but the act of taking fish from water was not considered paramount to killing them, they died spontaneously. Actually this creed aimed at the extinction of the human race, by which means only heaven could be regained. The Albigeois were also forbidden to take an oath. These last aspects of the religion struck at the very foundations of feudalism. The sect was persecuted with relentless virulence, and from the disturbances of its suppression arose that strange and beautiful fortress cathedral of Albi, the great red bastioned walls of which soar pompously upwards unbroken by the fretting of windows or the tracery of glass.

Janac was not positively *heretic*, but heresy had stained the immaculacy of her faith. Janac was not the scene of an inquisition, but she was penalized, if that can properly be called penalty which is to raise a long lasting monument and to create a work of art. The church so built is curious, a broad nave only—without pillars and with the most meagre of buttressing. A thin hexagonal tower rises to one side, topped with a pointed roof.

It is possible that the old leaven of heresy, still working, has made the villagers of the districts all about rather lazy in, if not antagonistic to, matters of religion. But the whole tract of land in this region is curious in matters of religion. A little farther to the south there are Protestant villages, and all over this country the struggles of the Catholics and Huguenots struck fire and sword.

They tell us that Martinolles, the village with the railway station nearest to Janac, voted her priest out of the place and shut up the church. Here we have a set of affairs different from those in England. The church is a public building, the priest no more than an official who may use it. The church, like the Mairie or the school, comes under the village council. Martinolles shut up the church; the priest had to go. Within six months Martinolles was begging the bishop to replace their spiritual adviser. Alas,

NEAR MARTINOLLES.

it was not because of any softening of Martinolles' heart— deprived of their priest they did not feel a lack of spiritual comfort, they remained athiest and unrepentant—but they soon discovered that without Sunday Masses to draw them to church the peasants did not come to Martinolles. The women—last devotees of Christianity, greatest purchasers of household provisions and wearers of Sunday frocks— went to other villages procuring at one and the same time

o

spiritual advice, kitchen necessities and the consolations of vanity. The tradesmen of Martinolles wanted Masses not for their souls but for their pockets.

But the *priestly* remedies for such unbelief have lost potency since the days when Janac church was built. Some of the mere choleric shepherds are, however, not remiss in brandishing their once terrifying crooks over the heads

THE SCHOOLMASTER'S WIFE AND GOAT.

of their recalcitrant sheep, anathemas and excommunications are laid in some villages upon the slightest excuse. Nor do the priests seem to perceive that they become a subject for bucolic jest in this matter. Nowadays the Jackdaw of Rheims could pilfer the whole cathedral treasures without the turn of a feather. Attendance at the *State* schools seems a very sore point with many of the clergy, in spite of the fact that instruction at the Church schools is often bad, and—owing to the Church's repudiation of many scientific theories—unsatisfactory.* But the worst crime (at least, so the peasant say) is the non-payment of the *culte*, the pew rent, as it were, the church (unauthorized) rate. The clergy are, in short, roundly accused of avarice; constantly one hears the remark: " Yes, he is good enough as priests go, and learned perhaps, but isn't he keen after the cash ? "

In this matter our mad priest, who lives over Potato's bottling cellar, is antagonistic to the appointed village *curé*. The mad priest is a strange-looking figure, he is tall and there is more than a hint of the Beethoven mask in his emphatic face. He goes dressed in the tattered remnants of priestly costume; his hat, as I have said, has the texture and colour of drowned kittens; his *soutane* hangs to a ragged edge; it is rent, repaired in some places with clumsy stitchings of string, in other places with pieces of sacking, while, through unmended gaps in what seems to be his only covering, one has glimpses of his flesh, to the scandal of the good wives of Janac. Much learning hath made him mad, but the villagers date his actual lapse from two incidents: the first, an appointment to give a discourse at Rome; the second, a present of an elaborately worked quilt from a nun in the convent. Probably the first made him realize that he was ambitious, the second—the quilt was, we have heard, a marvellous piece of work—showed him the treacheries of sex. At any rate, from that day he has renounced ambition, has renounced even comfort—his only relaxation an asthmatic accordion—and he will look no woman in the face. He lives on produce of his own garnering, every day sees him setting out with wheelbarrow and hoe, or toiling back bowed under a sack of potatoes or of beans or a load of brushwood.

* But has not the State of Texas recently passed an edict against teaching the doctrine of evolution within her boundaries ?

 He owns the house which backs on to Potato's beer shed, but lives in the attic. He has rich relatives who used to send him presents— chickens, ducks, rabbits and so on—but he always laid the offering on his doorstep for the first passer-by to take away.

His madness has, in fact, turned him to an austerity which, we must confess, seems very like Christianity. Fifteen hundred years ago he would have been revered, to-day he is a mark for the poked fingers of mingled admiration, pity and ridicule. His madness— but is he mad? They call him mad because, in his life, he seems to deny the value of everything which is generally counted as valuable; but half the Saints in the catalogue were twice as mad as he— Stylites and Anthony and all those old meditative Christians who retreated from Alexandria to caves upon the desert's edge—a million hermitages in a hundred lands attest to a similar piety which once was venerated.

"*Tiens,*" they say nowadays, "*il est fou ce prêtre-là; et, vous savez, montrer la cuisse aux dames, ça n'est pas chic.*"

Yet that old-time asceticism has its disadvantages in modern life. It *is* disturbing to reflect that Charlemagne was not immaculate, and that Sapho scratched her head for reasons other than a halting verse. Our modern Saint has a similar drawback, and has been interdicted from officiating at Mass in the Janac church for reasons purely

THE CHURCH OF JANAC.

hygienic. Nowadays most people would amendate the three Christian virtues into " Faith, Soap and Charity, and the greatest of these is Soap."

The banishment of this priest from the altar may nevertheless be as much a mark of jealousy as of outraged cleanliness. The village *curé* has naturally followed the normality of mankind : his fees have risen with the falling franc. But our hermit still clings to the former prices ; he is, in fact, a blackleg in more senses than one. That trade union, the Church, would boycott him. But the peasant who does not desert his economical habit even on the brim of death is satisfied, if not eager, to get to heaven as cheaply as possible, he would buy his extreme unction at bargain prices : thus our hermit is in some demand by sick-beds to the detriment of the *curé's* pocket. And so we come back to the peasant's accusation, that the modern *curé* is at best a tradesman, a would-be monopolist. The villagers are willing to be taxed for the policeman who keeps their social manners in orders, but are reluctant to pay priestly taxes : heaven is such a speculative affair to a man in health.

Undoubtedly the *curés* are often tradesmen, often they are bigoted, which gives them the air of tradesmen. Most are men of little birth, peasant sons striving for a cheaply won importance, or orphans brought up by the nuns in the shadow of the cloister educated on condition. There was in Janac no evidence that the priest stepped an inch beyond his official and his paid-for duties, no one offered him tribute beyond that he was an " instructed " man.

While writing the above it occurred to me to check our observations by a direct reference. Valentine, our charwoman, was polishing the parquet floor, so I asked her :

" Valentine, are you *Parisienne ?* "

Valentine : " No, monsieur. I come from the country. Not far from Paris, it is true, still from the country."

Myself: " What do they say of the *curés* in your parts ? "

Valentine (making a face and shrugging her shoulders): " Ah, well, monsieur, one is devout in my country. *I* am not devout; but, in general, yes."

Myself: " All parts are not alike ? "

Valentine (with an expressive flourish of the hand down her not very ornate person): " Ah, well, monsieur, in the country, you know, one is devout, forcedly. After all, the church, you know, it is the sole method of showing off one's dresses. There's the 14th of July, the people's feast, but otherwise—well, one doesn't ordinarily dress, not in the country. And so one is devout. One goes to Mass—to show one's self—what ? Of course one isn't exactly *devout*. But in Paris, for example, one doesn't need such occasions for dressing up."

Myself: " And the men ? "

Valentine: " Well, yes, the men are devout too. They go to Mass and then they go to the *buvette* to drink a glass or two, and it's odds on that they don't come home to lunch. Oh yes, they are also devout."

Myself: " And what do they think of the *curés* ? "

Valentine: " Oh, the *curés*. . . . "

She said no more, but her thoughts were working so furiously within her that the parquet in that square yard shines more vividly than in any other.

Our concierge, on the other hand, says that in her district —the French Pyrenees—the people are really devout; she adds: " No man in the village would dare to stay away from Mass." The cook of our little *bistro* restaurant also assures us that the people of her district are very devout too, the priests excellent men. This is in the Cantal. However, we have found out that her cousin is a priest, so perhaps we may discount her evidence as prejudiced. The truth seems to be that France varies considerably in different districts. One must be wary of generalizing from one source only.

The most remarkable of priestly figures in this district had died a few years before our visit. He was, if rumour is to be credited, a Friar Tuck of a Christian, a Friar Tuck who had found no Robin Hood. A jolly companion, poet, raconteur, who did not despise his glass. His verses in patois have become celebrated in the country, though to tell the truth they seem but narrative verse saved from doggerel by being in an unhackneyed tongue. He had a large nose, and when his statue was erected in Francheville the riotous youth of the place did him the honour of breaking the nose off. Here is a paraphrase of one of his stories :

Gondoulin, the most expert at knavery in all Segala, had educated his son to the like trade. One night, the two having set off to steal a sheep, came to the church wall of Clapier, where Gondoulin said to his son, " Wait here for me, close to the cemetery ; there will be less risk if I go alone." The lad clambered up on to the cemetery wall, and to pass the time began to crack and to eat walnuts which he had been carrying in his pocket. It happened on this very evening that Jambel, the sexton, a simple, lazy fellow, strong as a winepress, was late in coming to ring the Angelus. As he neared the cemetery wall he heard the sound of cracking nuts, and being superstitious and a coward by night he at once imagined that the devil was within crunching up the bones of the poor corpses. Half dead with terror he hurried off to the house of the *curé*.

" You are an ass," cried the *curé*, laughing.

But Jambel's evident terror was more expressive than

rhetoric, his eyes, his gestures, his throttled voice moved the priest, who said:

"Jambel, listen. If I hadn't got the gout I'd come with you, to show you, idiot that you are, that Satan doesn't need to munch us and to prove to you, my good fool, that you are drunk."

"Me! Drunk!" cried Jambel, and before the *curé* could protest he had gathered up the priest pick-a-back and was running off with him to the cemetery.

The son of Gondoulin heard him coming, saw in the darkness the figure of a man with something on his back; and, mistaking it for his father with a stolen sheep, cried out in a thin harsh voice:

"Is he fat?"

"Fat or thin, here he is," replied the bell-ringer, half crazy with fear. "O God, save him, or my poor *curé* is lost without remedy"; cast the priest to the ground and took to his heels with cries of terror.

Isn't it remarkable how the Church, above all other professions, loves to make a jest of its own members? A curious self-consciousness!

I think that there is something of a parable in this story; not, indeed, that the worthy *chanoine* saw it as anything but a humorous incident, peasant in its grotesque wit. But the picture of the peasant—frighted of the devil, catching up the Church and carrying it off on his shoulders, since the Church was too rheumatic to advance alone—has something justly applicable. The Church seems somewhat eager to be carried. It is the old story of autocracy, so often repeated. The autocrat cannot understand the duties or limitations of a constitutional monarch ; he thinks that a little firmness, a few decisive gestures, will seat him on the throne once more ; while, in truth, he is in danger of getting his head cut off. Rome cannot understand that where she once went proudly she must go now with hat in hand. Excommunications in this part of the world are, so 'tis said, commoner than tabby-cats, and anathemas are two a penny. The *curé* is, unfortunately for himself, in conflict with his cure ; he is in conflict because he has difficulty in getting payment of his church fees ; he is in conflict because he is in opposition to the State schools ; he is in conflict because he is reluctant to give up his old authority, he wishes to enforce Church rule over an insubordinate people. He is watched, spied upon and countered at every turn ; moreover, he has become a political factor and the fear of overwhelming Church influence plays a great part in holding off the vote from the women ; the sex which is notoriously " devout."

Also the *curé* suffers because of his celibacy. As soon as the Church ceases to be an autocracy, it must become a courtier. It must gain its authority in as many diverse ways as possible, like any vote-catching politician. It must act socially, educationally, benevolently and politically.

Socially the *curé*—bachelor, cut off in his little vicarage, seeking refuge from life in books or in the monstone of his breviary—is at a disadvantage, he is more or less out of touch with a full half of his parishioners' intimate interests. Educationally, compelled to enforce dogmas of the Middle Ages in a civilization of materialism, he is out of fashion. Benevolently, the chief paths for touching the peasants are taken over from him by the nuns, who are the visitors, the condolers, the sick nurses ; and these nuns by their very constitution are separated from the *curés* and absorb the gratitude, the sympathy and the spare humanity of the villagers and farm people. All the varied interests, feminine and humane, which in an English village the clergyman's wife concentrates into the family, are here by the nuns dispersed away from the clergy.

It may be noted that we have almost neglected the religious aspect of the Church; the fact seems to be that religious in the Christian sense the peasant is not, nor perhaps ever has been anywhere except perhaps in Slavonic lands. The worship of the country-side is still essentially pagan, it is composed of magic and of devil worship; the man who builds a fortress confesses himself afraid, so the peasant in worshipping is often confessing only to a terror of the devil. Christianity is only 2000 years old, it has not yet been seriously tried as a religion.*

But the devil-worshipping aspect of Christianity is losing its force; whether it is giving place to a real religion, may be a question. We were in Janac when the *curé* set out in full canonicals to bless the animals of the village. In our little triangular *place* was a healthy community of beasts; the Sestrols had two dogs, one cat, thirteen ducks, and a horse; at Tuk-Tuk's were the sausage-like pigs, a dozen hens, five rabbits, six little ducks and Cora, the pup; the baker owned two pigs; Lemoule and the cooper had five ducks, a pig, a hen with eight chickens, Oursa, the dog, and a donkey; in the stables which formed one side of the *place* were two draught oxen and a few chickens. The priest arrived with some ceremony, an acolyte bearing the mortar full of holy water, and the pestle with which to scatter the holy drops. But of all the menagerie only two pigs were

* Though, of course, the peasant does not admit this: even when he is anti-clerical he is less often anti-Christian. An unconscious agnosticism cover the more advanced thinkers, an unconscious devil-worship *comprises* the rest.

mustered to benefit by the consecrated dew. The fear of the devil being departed from Janac, gone was any enthusiasm for blessed meat, unhallowed animals went into the Janac stewpans and grease pots this year.

In the rest of the village things were little better, only

BLESSING THE ANIMALS.

one pig in the steep street which owned dozens; in the Place de Grifoules, standing between the tall ancient ironwork cross and the new marble *monument de guerre*, the *curé* made vague gestures at large, with the *aspersoir*, which gathered in but two pigs and one sheep; and a cat which was there by accident.

* *
*

The nuns have absorbed, away from the *curé*, the gratitude and sentiments of the villagers. He admonishes, they sympathize ; wherein is a great difference. While we were in Janac orders were sent down that a nun who had been in residence thirty-six years was to move elsewhere. Whether the rule came from the Church itself or from the State we did not ascertain, but there seems to be a regulation that after a certain period the sisters are thus painfully uprooted and sent to wither in other ground. Poor woman, for two generations she had spent her efforts on the village and now at this declining period of her life, when new attachments were almost impossible to make, when severance from old ones was like a sword stroke at the heart, she was dismissed. Her grief was almost equalled by that of the villagers. At the births of many she had presided, had doctored their infant maladies, had soothed their growing pains, physical, spiritual and educational.

Jo came into contact with the nuns across the chemist's piano. It had been borrowed by the sisters of charity for an entertainment which delighted the village for two nights at the Church school, an entertainment which was voted *almost* as good as the State school's cinema. The Church school being only a few yards away from our stable bedroom, Jo begged permission from the chemist's good-humoured wife to practise on the piano while it was so convenient, the schoolboys being on holiday. Her practising led to a request that she would play a solo at the entertainment, a request which, in view of the idiosyncrasies of the piano, she firmly declined to grant.

The entertainment itself was remarkable. On the first night the entrance to the school-house was crowded by the envious children of the anti-clericals, children who gazed with saddened faces at the passing files of their more fortunate companions, children suffering, with protest, for the political views of their parents. Inside we took our seats upon benches at the back, amongst the populace, to the grave amazement of the aristocracy—the doctor, the chemist, the tax-collector, the *huissier*, the lady from the château and others—which, arrayed in its most splendid attire, crowded forward as far as it was able, spreading over a large area of the already overheated room—it was full midsummer—a gas cloud of cheap scent, which we were only too glad to exchange for the more human odours of our companions.

The first part of the show was given by trained schoolchildren. The second part consisted of a play acted by girls of from sixteen to eighteen years old. It represented the fall from virtue to vice with an almost Hogarthian frankness, including a scene in a bawdy-house.

When the play was over, after thunderous applause, the *curé* rose and added his serious and orthodox voice to the lesson inculcated by the play. He warned his audience in no unmeasured tones on the dangers of light literature and especially those weekly publications costing from fifty centimes or less. We came to a tentative conclusion that the play missed its point owing to an ambiguous quality in the second act, those members of the audience sufficiently sophisticated to know what the second act implied were not likely to be much degenerated by cheap romance, while those who were totally mystified by the act were left wondering what the girl *had* done and how the novelettes had culminated in the almost dreadful end. Besides, there were three or four women in the village who *had* sacrificed their virtue at one time or another without evil consequences—indeed, one or two had done rather well out of it. They were not ostracized, and theory represented by the play must have ill harmonized with the practice of real life.

In any case the show produced by the nuns of Janac would scarcely have been passed by the London Censor of Plays, who stopped *Mrs. Warren's Profession* and *The Showing Up of Blanco Posnet*.

The play had one curious sequel. Although the chief actress had probably but the vaguest ideas of the sins she was supposed to be committing or to have committed, she played her part with a tragic intensity, an eloquence, and a sense of the drama wholly remarkable in a girl who may never have seen a play in her life. We could not help commenting to the Sestrols with enthusiasm on her performance. Our words, of course, were taken up and carried on without loss of emphasis; until the report reached the ears of the horrified priest that the English artists had said that the girl was a wonderful genius and that she should without fail take the train forthwith to Paris and storm the Parisian stage. The poor man went about for days trembling lest his little morality play should have turned inside out, and, owing to malignant heretic influence, should have produced the very result that he had been warning his flock against.

It was during the time of rehearsals that Jo came into contact with the nuns of the village. The Mother Superior was a sweet-faced woman gently ripened by the warm sun of retirement to a kindly middle age. After one or two meetings she became quite affectionate, and then her humane mind turned with regret to the idea that a person so apparently nice as Jo must go down into everlasting perdition. She was distressed. She could envisage with resignation that the millions of heretics unknown to her should flame in the hereafter; but that one of her acquaintance should thus suffer—no, it was horrible. One day, accompanied by the tall young girl who played the sea-green degenerate, the nun expressed her thoughts to my wife.

"Is it true that you are heretic?" she asked. "You repudiate the Blessed Virgin?"

"That is not accurate," answered Jo. "Protestants believe in the Virgin as much as you do, but do not accord to her as great an importance as they do to the Trinity."

"And you do not go to confession?" said the nun with wide-open eyes.

"We do not believe that a person can shelve the responsibility of his sins by confessing," replied Jo. "We believe that each carries his own sins and that he cannot so easily shed the burden."

"*Mais*," cried the young girl enthusiastically, "is that not a courageous creed, then?"

The nun reflected for a while.

"But," she hazarded at last, "yours is one of the—well, respectable religions, isn't it? You *may* be saved perhaps." She paused. "Still," she said primly, "you must admit that ours is the only true faith." She stole a sideways look at Jo and broke out into a delightful laugh, "Though of course you wouldn't admit it, naturally."

We wonder if the young girl confessed this conversation, and if she did, what penance was put upon her for her heresy.

XI

MAGIC AND MEDICINE—HEALTH AND HYGIENE

THE instinctive credence in magic and a half-hidden fear of the devil which are visible in the peasant's religion pursue him naturally into his medicine. Dr. Saggebou is sub-consciously held as one-half professional man and one-half wizard. When the people think that the wizard half of him is not sufficiently potent in spells they get to wizarding on their own account.

Dr. Saggebou himself represented the rising element in peasant society. It illustrates sufficiently the gap between English social ideals and those of France to say that Dr. Saggebou's father had been the postmaster, his grandfather a labourer. His brother was the chemist and, although the two played into one another's hands professionally, socially they were hardly upon speaking terms; not from inequality, for the chemist is as well considered as the doctor, but from incompatibility of humour, especially, I believe, between the womankind.

The doctor was a thickset, roughly dressed man nearing the fifties, with a lumbago limp, he had a forceful face, eyes set in moulded lids and an expanse of grey beard; the beard still gives an importance in France. Incurably loquacious, Dr. Saggebou had talked himself into the disapproval of his fellow villagers; so that his good qualities do not get the tribute which they merit. He was a know-all. There are beards which are aggressive and those which are defences;

beards which are as masked batteries and beards which are as smoke-screens. The doctor's beard was of the aggressive sort, you could not have beavered him. Mostly, nowadays, beards are grown by timid men to hide behind, as fawns hide in jungles; but the doctor's beard had a wiry intensity, and suddenly it would gape like a hidden porthole to let out volleys and carronades of assertion. The doctor was no fool, but he did not perceive the limits of wisdom; he dinned his cleverness into the peasants' ears until his cleverness went sour on them and became an exaggerated folly.

It was to the doctor that we owed the acacia trees which made a shady alley from the Hôtel Sestrol as far as our bedroom over the stable; the doctor, too, planted the acacias in the Place de Grifoules. He alone had perceived that Janac might be made into a show village for the summer if only the villagers would fit up accommodation for visitors. There were empty reparable houses by the dozen, but nobody bestirred himself. Indeed, the Hôtel Quemac up in the faubourg, in opposition to the doctor, had cut its own throat only for jealousy.

Janac village is curious in that it extends in length without breadth: it is a street a mile long, the post office is at the one extremity, and anybody living near the church has a two-mile walk to register a letter. The doctor, being Mayor at the time the post office was so placed, wished to plant the building near the market hangar, between it and the Hôtel Sestrol, in fact. But at this the faubourg rebelled. " The market, the Mairie and post office in the lower village," it cried (though the market-place is nearer to the faubourg than to the church). " That will make the lower village much too important. No, *we* must have the post office." Monsieur M.—proprietor of the Hôtel Quemac—then offered a large empty house almost next to his hotel, for a ridiculous rent; and the parsimonious village councillors, overruling the Mayor, planted the post office where it now is, in the hotel-keeper's empty house. Result, the hotel, which has only four bedrooms, turned away nearly thirty visitors seeking rooms this summer.

_{*}

The doctor has, with some difficulty, reduced by a large percentage the deaths in childbirth. When he started practice it was the custom to couch the expectant mother upon the filthiest materials which could be found in the house, or even in the stables; it needed all his arts to dissuade the peasant from this custom. But in spite of the fact that the French country doctor's main practice consists in hygiene and midwifery, Dr. Saggebou's true enthusiasm is not in medicine. He has the surgeon's instinctive contempt for pottering about the human organism, his is the *reductio* method, though petty surgery has his more special interest. I have described how he set the boy's leg in the street before the Sestrols' hotel; it is a further point of his character that he refused fees for the operation. " That peasant gave me loaves of bread during the war, good bread, when decent flour was unobtainable," he said to us. But he will use no magic, and so in some cases the patient goes to a more mysterious practitioner. The baker, for instance, with his consumption, visits a young doctor in Francheville, one who brandishes electricity, X-rays and threats of radium against his tuberculi. But how can magic cure the baker under the conditions in which he lives? Dr. Saggebou sees clearly that the man is doomed in the present circumstances. The baker lives in a typical Janac home, stone walls and tile floors exude a dankness even during the drought, the beds are often built into the walls or under the staircases and are surrounded by curtains, so that, though the baker ventures to open his windows a crack, he smothers himself in his cupboard or his tent of a bed. The beasts of the house, pigs and chickens, live in the cellars from whence their effluvia penetrates persuasively. How can the baker conquer his instinctive fear of nocturnal air? We who slept frankly with windows flung ajar were the object of incessant remonstrance from our hosts and from other well-disposed persons. I don't believe that even the doctor himself sleeps with the windows open. It is extraordinary how pig-headed humanity is against common sense in any branch of advancement, how it has resisted common sense in medicine, politics, education, and even in humanity, how we laugh at our ancestors for the common sense they have resisted and how we too resist common sense in our turn.

But the peasants still demand magic in their medicines as they demand it in their religion; indeed, a little farther to the southward, in Spain, an incantation to a Saint is often held as more efficacious than the science of the doctor, as maybe with some Spanish doctors, it is. We have already instanced Madame Sestrol's firm belief that Lourdes held the major merit in the curing of Raymond; and we had a further instance very soon after our arrival. Monsieur Sestrol told us how he had been cured of rheumatism. The illness was so bad that he could scarcely move, far less work:

doctors had practised on him without giving relief. By chance he heard of some wise woman who had a miraculous cure. He was hoisted into a cart, was driven to her house, bargained with her for her recipe and actually paid her fifty francs, a large sum before the war, for the prescription. He says that he concocted the potion according to instruc-

THE OLD MILL OF JANAC.

tions, drank it—" *il fallait avoir l'estomac fort pour avaler ça* "—and in three days was cured. He had afterwards given the prescription to the nuns, so he said, and with it they had cured numberless persons. He could not remember the ingredients, except the first instruction, which gives a clue to the nature of the whole, "Take a bucketful of water and boil it until it is reduced to half the quantity."

He also said that one could prevent a burn from blistering if immediately after the accident one breathed upon the injured part, making the sign of the cross at the same time. The old father of Monsieur "Chestnuts," who had had some local reputation as an amateur magician, averred that he had done this several times with invariable success. Sestrol had a jest—well in his manner—that once a sufferer had been hurried to Père "Chestnuts" for cure, but that, having discovered where the burn was, he declined to operate. The man had sat down upon a red-hot poker.

The Church is connected with magic medicine even more closely than in this competition between the curative properties of saintly vows and materia medica. There are always a series of quack medicines offered to the public under the signature of the *abbé* so-and-so, or the *abbé* this-and-that. Why *abbés* should be considered so enlightened in medicine has only one explanation, the magical one which embraces both Church and Doctor. There is a famous *abbé* quack in Toulouse, who although he has been condemned several times by the French courts to prison, still continues to hold the faith of and to gull the peasants.

We do not know whether it may not be in exasperation against these priestly incursions into his profession, that Dr. Saggebou is a virulent anti-clerical. The Church retorts upon him by confounding anti-clerical and anti-Christian in the minds of the faithful; and so the more devout of the peasants cling to the services of the other doctor who, though having the virtues of devotion, is admittedly less able than the loquacious ex-mayor.

* * *

The peasant houses, which are like grottos even in the drought, must be terrible places in the winter-time, when the

THE RIVER VALLEY FROM THE DOCTOR'S GARDEN

rain falls so fiercely that Janac street becomes a leaping torrent. Brushwood is their only means of heating these cavernous rooms, of which the windows and doors have already been misfitted by the sun. A device, peculiarly efficacious for women, is much used to preserve a personal warmth, a small charcoal box stove used as a footstool. But in the house of the baker, before he took it, this individual fire caused a tragedy. The wife of the previous *garde champêtre* was not a very sensible woman—is it the habit of *garde champêtres* to marry idiots ?—and she hit upon the economical idea of filling her footwarmer with compressed sawdust instead of charcoal, for compressed sawdust is often used here as a slow burning device for simmering. However, either the sawdust was not compact enough or there was a draught, but the sawdust flamed up and set fire to her flannelette petticoats. Material for a ruthless rhyme, indeed.

These peasant houses have a curious atmosphere, they are "workshop" houses made as though even rest were but a part of labour, and the articles within them have the air not of furniture, but of tools, the simplest possible fabrication to achieve the object. No hint of relaxation mars their severe utility, while even those things which are not so positively useful are still utilitarian in their aim : the calendar advertises some mixture for stopping leaks in old barrels, for instance. These persistent peasant workmen seem to envisage no holiday from work, sitting down to eat one's dinner is as much a business as cleaning out the cowshed, even the bed with its monstrous balancing eiderdown makes one think of poor old Atlas rather than of Morpheus. No, if the peasant wants relaxation he goes to the café where he drinks a glass of wine or plays a hand of manille. If the wife wants relaxation she balances a baby on her bosom, clasps a second by the hand, and lurches off to lean against a neighbour's doorpost and to gossip.

The houses of the village aristocracy are direct developments of the peasant furnishing, but they have lost their air of utility and gained nothing in comfort: it is as though a workman had encased the handles of his chisels and the box of his plane in figured velvet. In the doctor's house, for instance, there wasn't a room that we saw which did not scream discomfort both to the sense of touch and of vision. You could hardly imagine one of these rooms in use. The chairs were as repulsive as erections of rectangular wood and ornamental velvet well could be, the pictures attracted your eye only to jar your sense of harmony, the chimneypiece sprouted strange masses of tormented bronze representing semi-nude woman draped in raiments of distorted metal gesticulating over a monstrous attic clock surmounted by the head of Ajax. The floor was so polished that it was difficult to stand upon it; and amidst the discordances of colour even the cut flowers in a violet vase had been turned from beauty into yet one more discord.

Yet there is, in the French nation as a whole, a genuine and deep love of the visual arts.

The doctor was very proud of his bill of health during the drought. "No epidemics, no epidemics," he went about repeating as though epidemics were to be expected. "I tell you, *monsieur et dame*; Janac is the healthiest village in the healthiest part of France, which is the healthiest country in Europe, which is the healthiest continent in the world." He lived in the superlative relation, the little spring on the hill beyond his house was the purest water in France, better than Vittel, Vichy, etc., the purest in France, *i.e.* in Europe, *i.e.* in the world.

Still, we undeceived him on one point. He has a cause at heart; a cause which he had preached till the peasants yawned over the mere mention of it; a cause for which he had memoralized the Government—he read us his peroration—it was a demand for medical inspection of schools. "It will enlighten the world," he cried, and was very cast down when we told him that such an examination had long been the order in England.

But though the bill of health was good and though the atheist cobbler of the faubourg could only enjoy his favourite pastime of following funerals twice during our stay, we came to the conclusion that the index of lunacy for Janac must be significant of some serious deterioration. The *garde champêtre's* wife and mother-in-law both were on the distant limits of sanity, the commissionaire had been mad, the father-in-law of the man of position in Toulouse was weak-minded, the murderess was counted irresponsible, her husband had been also. The peasant called the " Wolf " was counted mad, so were two of his children, and the litigant ex-nun was clearly cracked. Sestrol had a story of a woman in the near vicinity who had gone mad in the train, a wild story compounded of madness and of tempest and of a four-mile walk wheeling the lunatic tied into a wheelbarrow;

one of Sestrol's fields was hired from the guardians of a man who had gone mad and who had split open his sister-in-law's head with a hatchet; and besides the mad priest there were two half-idiot children of the present generation who were continually in trouble in the streets, one had the Mongolian form of idiocy and went about looking like some small Chinese monster. These are the ones who spring to memory, there were others whom we have forgotten: but as it is, it stands no mean a record for a village of under one thousand inhabitants.

* *
*

Monsieur Saggebou, the chemist, was some years older than his brother, the doctor, and he was almost the opposite in every respect save that of geniality. The doctor had a claim to knowing everything, through which one suspected that he read nothing; the chemist was a furious reader and if he had knowledge did not parade it. He was first and foremost a musician, he was a musician of that nature which seems to the small boy so easy, he was a conductor. He played upon an orchestra, when he could get one; his sole other claim to musical capacity was a not very developed execution on the flute. Poor Monsieur Saggebou, he was at that moment deprived of his instrument, the village band, *le fanfare*, having been broken up as we have described by the *intransigeance* of the atheistic cobbler.

The chemist was a small, rotundish man, who wherever he went trailed a faint halo of asafœtida, this highly odorous and persistent gum being in constant demand for some of the mysterious drugs of a veterinary nature. He was like the fiftieth cousin of the man who had eaten the Popomack, and it is a genuine tribute to the charm of his society that his aura could not prevent us from seeking his company.

He was himself conscious of his social handicap. As we enter his shop he would glance guiltily, smell his fingers, ejaculate " Peuh ! " rush into the interior of the house, wash, return with a grin, flash another sniff at his fingers, ejaculate " Peuh ! " once more, shrug his shoulders at the inevitable, and come genially forward offering a hand, odorous indeed, though not with galbanun, nor yet with frankincense or thyme.

His house faced the little common at the extreme end of Janac, near the hotel and the post office ; and you had to plunge through a garden filled with aloes, and shrubbery, and bold blossoming plants, so that one felt shy as though penetrating privacy ; you came into the chemist's shop as though paying a call rather than as a purchaser of pepsin tablets or of aspirin. Invariably one found a long, haggard, black-clad peasant waiting for some asafœtida drug, and small girl with two bottles of " mixture as before." The chemist seemed to be in many ways a rough-and-ready pharmacist, he emptied the drugs into his tainted hands and cast the superfluous back into the jars, so that we wondered whether all his mixtures did not contain faint flavour as of asafœtida. If they did the peasants probably ascribed a superior potency to them because of their nastiness. Behind him rows of jars in close regiments, inscribed with the strange names of forgotten medicaments in dog Latin, kept alive the old dim flavour of magic.

I suppose we feel inclined to flatter the chemist because

he flatters us a little with his admiration. His two passions, reading and music, coincide with ours, and his submerged desire is in strange accordance too: his dream is to have a caravan and go wandering through the by-ways of France. In this he is not French. He sees, perhaps, his caravan a little glowingly. So many stay-at-homes have said enthusiastically, "Oh, if I hadn't any ties, I would go wandering like you do," that we have become suspicious of these lie-abed wanderers. Wandering in the imagination is like creating Utopias. You can ignore three parts of human nature and make golden dreams with the other quarter. But we felt that the chemist was more sincere than the majority of these dream-travellers.

The chemist's wife was as good-natured and as kindly as her husband. She had, moreover, a queer tinge of race which was not evident in the other women of Janac, even in the women of the " aristocracy." She was like the squire's dame without the squire, or without the landed interest. Her son, a doctor in Brittany, had become a royalist. We don't know what motives swayed him to this queer political reversion, perhaps he would have felt a sympathy with a good old English snob who once said to my wife, " I'm so glad I'm English and not French, you know. I always feel it's *so common* to have a President instead of a King."

The chemist and his wife came nearest to what was Victorianism in England. Their library consists of sentimental books which they love and sensual books which they read but abuse. Of course, as soon as he heard the scandal about " *La Garçonne* " he bought it, cursed it roundly and pressed it on to us with energy. Paris floats in his mind as vague memories of student licence, Montmartre and the Concert Mayol. This is the general idea of Paris in the Provinces, and the provincial Frenchman seems to know even less of true Paris than the travelled foreigner. For instance, Lemoule took his wife to Paris for her honeymoon, the only thing she desired to see was the three-quarters nude actresses at the *Folies-Bergères*. When she had seen them she said that they didn't seem much to make a fuss about, their figures weren't so *very* good. Her remark illustrates a real French simplicity in reference to the nude figure, which seems to make so curious a contradiction when one hears that the nuns are shocked at English girls who don't wear a chemise in the bath.

* *
*

There are also remedies which the chemist does not sell, more homely peasant remedies which are not essentially magical in operation. The old fourteenth-century cure for wounds is still in common use. Swallows' nests boiled are counted amongst the best of poulticings, and fresh-cut sheep's wool is said to be an excellent counter-irritant for chest complaints. A stocking filled with hot wood cinders is a common-sense night wrap for a sore throat, for which one should also gargle with water in which blackberry shoots have been boiled. For swellings and especially for abscesses in the face a hot poultice of elder flowers was held to be marvellous; for the stings of wasps or of hornets the wax from the ear was recommended. For lumbago the sufferer was couched in bed with a bag of wheat, previously heated in the oven, laid over his back. For the *grippe* nothing was counted so efficacious as a cup of tea.

In general the French peasants treat tea as a violent drug. They have a number of "infusions," as they call them, camomile for the stomach's sake, *tilleul* to make one perspire, and so on. But the chief, most powerful, is tea. The peasant, however, does not waste his money on the article from China. I was walking one day with Raymond, to the fête at Martinolles, and at the side of our road were small purple flowers.

"*Tiens, Monsieur Jean,*" said Raymond, "that is tea."

"No," I replied; "tea grows in China and India."

"*Je le sais,*" answered Raymond, "but that is tea all the same. *Our* tea. It is much better than the Chinese article; besides, it costs nothing, while the other is very, very dear."

Other remedies are more disgusting, for the peasant mind often holds that the more offensive the more efficacious.

One can scarcely pretend to be honest in one's account of health and hygiene without attempting some indications of the sanitary arrangements of the village, touchy subject though it may be under the censorship of modern propriety. It would, perhaps, be better in general if this section were as curt as Horrebon's chapter on Snakes in Iceland, but a certain illumination of French character, more especially of Sestrol's character, is unveiled by a more expanded description.

When we first demanded of Monsieur Sestrol where was *le cabinet*, he was for a moment abashed and muttered a few stumbling sentences. He was not abashed for the reason that would have abashed an Englishman or an American, but his confusion arose from a sudden perception of the gap separating what he had to offer us from what we might expect. However, he recovered his aplomb with little delay, and making a generous gesture with his hand put the whole landscape at our disposal. This would seem to indicate that this section might have been as curt as Horrebon's, but there is more to come.

HEALTH AND HYGIENE

Many of the villagers were as primitive as the Sestrols, no doubt, but others were not. Here and there dotted about in the terraced gardens, sometimes in most public situations, were rickety sheds often lacking doors, and more often incompletely boarded, and for those who were completely destitute the commune had erected under an archway near to the Mairie a small building, the stink emanating from which made a nauseating barrage across the village street some ten yards from the doctor's house.

But our innocent query had stirred Sestrol's conscience. He decided to build us a *cabinet*. The job was undertaken in a manner thoroughly Continental, except that in his pride and ardour Monsieur Sestrol expended upon the erection far more money than the commune had upon that one for the populace. He also did it with a frankness which was very embarrassing to Jo.

In front of our stable-bedroom the road abutted on a terrace some ten feet deep, and here, in the full light of the most extreme publicity, Sestrol planned his improvement. He first imported three capacious cement drainpipes which he set on end reaching from the bottom to the top of the terrace wall; these he solidly enclosed in masonry, but, as he was his own mason and as his leisure was but limited, the job took the whole duration of our stay to complete. These pipes were for a primitive cesspool. Naturally, his operations aroused interest and crowds of curious villagers and all the visiting farmers came to question the motives of his strange architecture. To all of which we, from our room, could hear Sestrol's proud reply :

"*Je suis en train de fabriquer un cabinet pour les Anglais, quoi ?*"

The building went on long enough to keep us blushing, but—on the immediate approach of our departure—is still incomplete. However, Sestrol does not consider his time wasted. He is so pleased with us—we say it without false shame—that he is hopeful of catching other English guests for next summer. They are to benefit from our inconveniences. A few days ago, Sestrol said :

"*Tiens, Monsieur Jean.* How does one translate *cabinet* into English ? "

We told him ; we wrote it out. Then we asked what motive he had.

" I will paint it clearly on the door," he answered, " and then other English visitors, seeing it, will come to stay with us."

A Sestrolian reasoning—does he not dub himself *débrouillard ?*—and yet we wonder. To most English travellers except to the most hardened—such as ourselves—that door, on the main road itself, will have an air of most intercipient publicity.

XII

. . . AND THE FRUITS IN THEIR SEASONS

WHEN we arrived we were picking wild strawberries at the railside; now, that we are on the point of departure, we have already cleared the Sestrol's pergola of all its white grapes. There only remain the diseased maroon bunches and the little black ones which "taste like bugs" but which make excellent wine. We have seen the summer from its beginning to its end, the acacias have passed from bloom to the sere, the yellow leaf, the first walnuts have come in, hard shelled, damp and bitter, only the chestnuts sealed in their hedgehog husks are still profiting by the yet warm autumnal sun.

We have seen out all the fruits of the country-side and yet we have lacked for fruit. The end of the strawberry season left a gap till the plums came in, for currants do not grow here and the gooseberry is almost unknown in France. With the plums Janac station began to pile up with Covent Garden baskets and the village speculators asked us daily about the value of the "livre steerleeng." Here they do not repine for the depreciation of the franc. Hard on the heels of the plums come the peaches and the melons; and the mushrooms, though not precisely fruit. Your Southern peasant gourmet is a connoisseur in mushrooms. *Petit Larousse* depicts twenty-three edible varieties; and terrifying things some of these appear, the Amanite family being a large one with the disadvantage that many of its edible varieties are closely imitated by poisonous brethren. The Amanite *golmelle* looks like an umbrella made of an old British shield, but the Amanite *fausse golmelle* also awaits the hardy but not too perspicacious glutton. There is the *lactaire délicieuse*, the delights of which may prove too late to be those of the *lactaire roux* or the *lactaire vénéneux*. How the peasant dares to go a-mushrooming I cannot imagine, but dare he does, and year after year takes its toll of the reckless harvester. Luckily for us the Sestrols offered us none but fungi of long appreciated honesty, huge flabby cepes, and the ordinary *champignon* of which they spoilt the flavour be steeping it in boiling water before frying.

Janac was exporting plums to England, yet we had difficulty in getting plums to eat. Your Southerner has no true appreciation of fruit, which gathered before it is ripe has a devastating effect upon childhood; and, once having bitten twice shy, so to speak. To those around Janac fruit existed for the purposes primarily of making drink, all the joys of luscious ripeness were bartered for the products of the distillery. Offer a Janaquois a plate of plums purple with the bloom upon them, their silken skins slashed and showing the golden tissue of their rich content; he will murmur " Plum brandy "; offer Raymond Sestrol a bunch of ripened grapes and he reaches out for the *chopine* of *piccolo*. With some difficulty we persuaded Madame Sestrol to stew us fresh yellow plums for a lunch dish; she tried them once, said they were delicious, but preferred her mess of prunes, half mouldy, half rotten, her own curing. Only the melon, *cantaloup* or *pastèque*, did they really value because of its fresh sweetness. The apples they turn to Calvados, even the sloes which cluster thick in the hedges are sometimes gathered to go into the distilling vats and to exhale their strength, not their sweetness, through the copper

... AND THE FRUITS IN THEIR SEASONS

coils of the *bouilleurs de cru*. In the early winter the distillers come and plant their stills on the roadside near to the Sestrols' *remise*, and the plums, sloes, apples and grape skins, after having degenerated into foul rottenness for some months, are here concentrated into translucent soul-snatchers of various denominations. In those days a drink of raw spirit is to be had for the asking, the distillers sup the liquor as is runs from the still-pipe. In this period of the year the grave-digger is gay and full of spirits.

***

The drinks of the country-side, though they do not emulate the complexity of those of the town-dwellers, and though the peasant has natural appetite enough to need no *apératif*, are nevertheless of a far wider range than any used by our English yokel. Whisky and gin the peasant does not know, there are full many enough fruits which yield alcohol to debar them from turning good grain into spirit. There is the Calvados from the apples ; the Cognac from the vine ; the Marc from the grape skins ; plum brandy from the plums and sloes. There are the well-known liqueurs, such as Curaçao, Benedictine, Crème de Menthe, and a number of modern inventions, such as Raspail or Izarra, or a weird peppery invention of some distiller of Toulouse named " China." After one visit to his wholesale merchant Sestrol came back with an especial treat for the feast time, a bottle of transparent liqueur in which small particles of gold leaf fell like glittering snow in a sluggish atmosphere, *eau-de-vie de Danzig*. Cocoa spirit is the woman's drink *par excellence*. Though in general the peasant stuck to his wine, he often finished off his meal with a fillip from one of these alcoholic luxuries. In any case he took his coffee strengthened with a dash of cognac ; indeed, coffee without cognac was hardly counted as coffee. For the commercial travellers, artists, and fainéants generally who might need appetite stimulation, the Sestrols kept a heavy wine flavoured with quinine, which had the not very seductive name of " Byrrh " ; or a decoction of liquorice called " *Goudron* " (tar) which was usually drunk mixed with lemon or blackcurrant syrup diluted with soda water.

_{*}

The walnuts which now clothe only the northern slope of Janac peninsula, but which were formerly in great abundance, give rise to another concoction, which stands half-way between drink and medicine, *eau-de-noix*. It is made with the green nut, at the period when we would gather them for pickling, and anybody who had been making *eau-de-noix* could hardly conceal the fact since her hands and arms would be stained a rich walnut from the exuded juices. *Eau-de-noix* needs such an intimate handling of the material. The nut has to be rubbed down to pulp on a grater and this pulp is then mixed with alcohol and allowed to stand. The fluid is counted as an almost universal elixir, something, one gathered, in the nature of Don Quixote's *bálsamo de Fierabrás*.

The walnut has lost its pre-eminence in the country nowadays. Few of the women tinted themselves to make up this elixir, though the *garde champêtre's* wife went about looking like a tattooed Indian for several weeks, having not only stained her hands and arms, but having further rubbed her reckless fingers across her face. But before the railway and cheap transport came the walnut took the place which the olive of the South fills to-day. Walnut oil was a considerable product of these Aveyronnais hills, and we got by chance one of the large, beautiful, red earthen pots in which the walnut oil was carried. Shortly before our arrival Sestrol had bought a farm in the valley, and only during the time of our stay did he think of examining the loft of his new property. Here he found rolled into a corner three old earthen walnut oil-jars, jars long gone out of use in the country. One, the most ancient, a Roman-looking vase, was badly broken and caked an inch deep in layers of old dried oil, but the second in size was perfect, with a queer clay stopper. Wondering somewhat at our desiring such an outworn object, he made us a present of the jar, which with some difficulty we transported, in a rucksack, back to Paris, where it now reposes in our studio on a long bookcase, between a huge old basin of Seville and an equally large vinegar bottle of blown olive-tinted glass.

* * *

One day in late June we were wandering. The heat was intense but invigorating, with a sun which was baking in spite of a sky flecked with mackerel clouds.

They say here:

"Ciel pommelé
N'a pas grande durée,"

but in Janac the weather prophets had no honour, they had the signs all off by heart, sure enough, but the weather refused to be guided by them. However, there was a cool bottom to the wind, and it was a perfect day for a walk, so we went cheerfully exploring the outlying country for views. The landscape of hill and of dale was rather monotonous, for the hills were clothed with chestnut and walnut trees and between them the grasslands and corn-lands were not yet changed in colour. Still, there were vineyards, and the mere presence of the vine has a spirit of luxury and romance to us chilled Northerners.

Such a vineyard came down to the roadside. It was

planted in prim rows. The stem of the vine was pruned off close to the ground, so that the new shoots made of the plant a low shrub more like a gooseberry-bush than that clinging parasite which nature had designed. But the transformation of the vine was yet incomplete. The vine to-day is somehow like a woman, it is as much like its prototype as a painted, corseted, low-waisted woman is like Mother Eve. The waist of the vine had been cut down; its flexible shape had been remoulded; and now the process of *maquillage* was being proceeded with, but with this difference: woman paints herself to attract, man paints the vine to discourage, parasites. To and fro amongst the vines a man was tramping. A broad rush hat shaded his sun-stained face. He wore clothes of brown mottled with pale blue, on his back, like a knapsack, he carried a large copper canister which was stained like his clothes. As he went slowly between the ranks, the vines put off their delicate vesture of yellow green and reappeared vivid in pure cerulean. Here was a first cousin to the gardeners in *Alice Through the Looking Glass.* His paint-brush was an air spray, with his left hand he worked a lever which projecting from the canister produced the necessary air-pressure. By the roadside a barrel half hidden in the hedge contained the paint with which this gardener was reshaping nature to his heart's desire. We peered into the barrel. Within was a liquid which looked as though all the turquoises of Arabia had been liquefied and strained through the sky.

While we were thus gazing, rapt by that pure and magic blue, the peasant ceased his pumping—having exhausted his supply—and came towards us to replenish his canister from the barrel. We gave him " *Bon jour,*" and then for a while, in silence, watched him spooning up from the barrel this liquid jewel stuff, pouring it into the copper canister, recking nothing of the peculiar emotional qualities of its colour, little realizing that to an artist he was almost committing sacrilege. He rested his canister on the edge of the barrel and looked at us and smiled.

"It is heavy," we said, indicating the canister.

THE SULPHATER.

"As for that," he returned, "if there is a job it's got to be done."

"You are changing nature a bit," we said.

An English labourer would not have understood, but the Latin culture breeds a quicker wit.

"A bit," he agreed, "*c'est le métier, quoi?* You have not seen sulphating before?"

"No," we answered.

"Then you have no vines in your country?"

"Nowadays, no. Rich people grow grapes in houses built of glass and heated by stoves, but outside, the vine will ripen no longer."

He opened his eyes at this, the idea of building glass houses and heating them with stove in order to grow a few grapes was beyond the stretch of his imagination. Possibly he thought us to be lying, as an English peasant might think if he were told that the Laplanders were building greenhouses to grow turnips.

"Once," we went on, "the vine did grow in England, we had local wines. But the climate has changed."

"*That's* true," said the peasant, glad to be back into the regions of recognizable veracity. "Why, we used to have proper summers and winters. But now everything has got mixed up. We get bits of summer in the middle of winter, and bits of winter in the middle of summer. Nowadays there's never snow in the village, and once we used to get some every winter. And then look at the change in vine cultivation. When I was a lad we never did this sulphating, it wasn't necessary. We ploughed the vines once or twice and that was an end of it. Now, what with the phylloxera, and what with these blights like we had yesterday, one is never at an end of work, nor of cost. It's work, work, work, and spend, spend, spend, all the time. And then, after all your work and expense, it rains in the summer as it never used to rain, and the water gets into the grapes, and in consequence the wine is so weak that we can scarcely sell it, so that they have to import strong wines from Spain and mix it up. But that mixed stuff isn't like drinking a proper pure wine. Or, if you don't get the rain, it's ten to one you get the hail, and just as your vines are ripe, down comes a hail storm and ruins the lot."

"But do you often get hail here?" we asked.

"In the last seven years my vines have been ruined by hail three times," said the man. "You see, the hail seems to come in regular streaks—like rivers—and each year it follows the same course as if it was running in a valley. There's a streak of hail comes from over there, and when it comes it always comes the same way."

"Then," we said, "you aren't satisfied with nature?"

"Oh, *la Nature*," answered the peasant, "she is a worn-out lunatic."

"So you change it," we went on, "and you paint it blue. There are people in Paris who believe the same, they are called Post-Impressionists."

"Post-Impressionists," said the peasant. "B——e, if I ever heard the name. Still, if that's what they are, I am one of them."

And he shouldered his canister and returned to his task of painting nature bright blue.

We too continued our way, and as we went we rejoiced yet more that there were these village post-impressionists who had the courage to alter the face of nature, who could give us these exquisite and strange areas of turquoise gleaming amongst the greens of the walnut woods and the gold of the corn.

*_**

The season of the vintage is heralded by the appearance in the street of large iron hoops and monstrous barrel staves; and in a trice the newsvendor is rebuilding his previously stowed vat, so is the blacksmith, and the ex-policeman master of Tambour. The cooper, come in from the fields, has now for some time been busy in his workshop, and clouds of smoke drifting round the corner of the triangular *place* show that he has a new barrel half finished, and that he is toasting the inside of it with a small bonfire in an iron basket, in order to make the new staves flexible for his descending hoops. A merry thudding, true drummer's prelude to a Toper's Chorus, is beaten on the staves and hoops of half a hundred tuns as Janac prepares to welcome the new grape harvest. One or two tractable wine-presses are dragged out from the seclusion of barns.

In the prim vineyards the pale blue of the copper has long ago been washed away by the autumnal rains, and here and there the vines are putting on their flamboyant cadmiums and vermilions, so that in another fortnight the hills will flame again more brightly than they did during the mountain fires. Already the sunbonnets are seen like large white distant flowers amid the green and gold of the vines, and into the village comes the patient donkey with half-tubs slung on either side, like panniers, heaped high with the grape.

We have been tarrying in the country-side for the vintage. A romantic spirit has made us wish to see the last wind up of the summer, the last harvest which still retains some of that gaiety, some of that simple humour of joy which, if old records speak truly, was the guerdon of every harvest, a joy which the mechanical reaper and the cutter and binder has successfully ousted from modern agriculture. But of a sudden we are going. A certain twist of humour urged us to stay; but we are not staying.

Sestrol has not been one of the village tub-thumpers. He builds no vat, for in the cellar he has built a cement well five feet deep into which his grapes are thrown. Though the wine-press is seen here and there, it is still the custom in

... AND THE FRUITS IN THEIR SEASONS 235

these parts to press the grapes as Father Abraham pressed his, with the feet, or rather with the whole body. The pictures of the East show us bronzed Hercules delicately dancing on the pressing *floor*, here the peasant strips to the 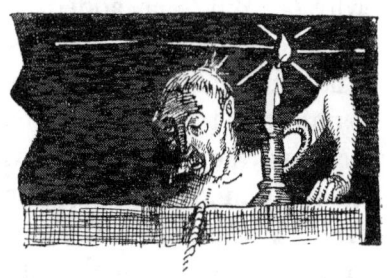 buff and leaps bodily into his vat. If he is a careful man he has an *aide* with a rope to fish him out in case of accident, for the carbonic fumes may overpower him ; but the peasant often by use becomes careless, as does the miner with dynamite. Each year several reckless spirits are asphyxiated in the local wine-pressings, drowned like our English prince, if not in Malmsey, in vintages of Burgundy, Touraine or Bordeaux. I confess that I was tempted to stay for the vision of Sestrol, like some huge pallid bull-frog, descending into his wine-vat, prancing at the end of the rope clutched in the anxious hands of Madame Sestrol or of Raymond. But I can imagine that, after all. I can imagine him emerging from the vat, his body all blushing, like that of Ariadne, from the embrace of Bacchus.

We had asked Lemoule one or two questions about this local wine making, questions which made Lemoule in his turn go a-questioning. He asked one of his acquaintances, " Do you wash before you go into the wine-vat ? " To which the peasant answered, with evident surprise, " *Mon Dieu*, why? But," he added, "I wash in warm water when I come out, naturally, because the wine is cold, you know." The wine making, if it no longer leads to orgies, if it no longer paints the town red, has still at least its ancient habit of painting the townsmen scarlet, for a period, at least.

Autumn, which loads the vine, brings out another strange fruit, *le chasseur*. The conditions of sport in France are true to their national motto, *Liberté, Egalité et Fraternité*: you are free to wander everywhere in pursuit of a red-legged partridge, all sportsmen are equal since only a gun licence is required, and the brotherhood exists even between sportsmen and game, since the gunner who cannot hit his bird or beast often pots his comrade. On the first week of the opening of *la chasse*, the newspapers reserve a column for accidents. After that period either the blood lust is assuaged or the public interest is exhausted.

I have often been perplexed by the problem of *Tartarin*. This book which so moves French readers to mirth failed to amuse me, and in general fails to amuse English readers. It seems as though tragedy is common to all countries, while humour is not properly interchangeable; we do not appreciate *Tartarin*, the French cannot understand *Alice in Wonderland*. The question of Alice is, we think, more subtle than that of *Tartarin*. We think *Tartarin* a silly book, we will admit absurdity as far as Mark Twain's *Tramp Abroad*, but thence on absurdity must be fantastic, not foolish, or it may be absurdity brought about by contact between unpractical man and recalcitrant nature, as so often occurs in *Three Men in a Boat*. Man merely dressing up and being an ass we find dull. But the fact is that *Tartarin* is not a foolish but almost a true book; Tartarin is not an absurd mannequin invented for farce, he is a serious Southern sportsman: the owner of the inhabitable château was spoken of with respect as "*un véritable massacreur de gibier*"; like the three doughtie men of the old part song he seemed to have sworn a mightie oath to slaye whate'er he met. History relates that on one occasion, exasperated at the end of a blank day, in order not to return empty-handed, he assassinated his neighbour's cock which was scratching in the hedge. But we are not here in the true region of Southern sport, it is farther to the south, in Toulouse, Gascony, and in Southern Languedoc that the character which the rest of France, as much as ourselves, considers to be flamboyant, childish even, is the most marked, where *Tartarin* is true. In Janac the sportsman is, on the whole, serious and often efficient.

The game consists of a few red-legged partridges, some hares, and *sauvage* rabbits, as well as a lot of miscellaneous small objects to be shot *at*, such as larks, sparrows, etc. There are also wild boars which do much harm to the crops and which are sometimes tackled with dogs. The peasants owe the wild boars to a landowner of the Vaour region who thought he would like to breed a few on his land for sporting purposes. But like so many importations the boars spread rapidly and are now becoming a serious pest in the country whence, owing to the thick patches of brush preserved for firewood, the animals cannot be exterminated.

We are leaving Janac chiefly for culinary reasons. After five months of veal and of goose grease we have engendered a beef-complex, we feel like Kipling's hero in *The Mark of the Beast*. But it is not only desire but fear which is driving us away. The new wine will soon be drawn from the spigot. Here they drink the wine as soon as it will run, and if one isn't used to it it does curious things to the stomach, let alone that Sestrol has bathed in it. We cannot face the new wine. Nor can we face the peculiar dish which goes with the new wine.

It is a dish common in Southern France and very popular in Spain; in the latter country they call it Baccala'o, here it is named sto-feece. This is cod-fish which has been salted and dried, it is strong meat with a flavour that makes one think of something which wanted to go bad but wasn't allowed to. We analysed sto-feece at last to its true derivation, stock-fish, the food which Polar explorers give to their dogs. The curious quality about sto-feece is that every cook admits that it is unappetizing stuff—as cooked by anybody else—but "as I cook it, m'sieu, that is another affair." Madame Sestrol pressed a dish of sto-feece upon us in spite of our protests, we could not eat it, though we admitted, falsely, that *her* method of cooking it was superior to any other we had experienced. Now sto-feece ("Stuffy," we call it) is the regulation accompaniment to new wine, and at the sound of the combination we shuddered, gave a hurried notice and packed our bags.

XIII

ADIEU . . . ADIEU!

WE are having our last supper. As a final send off they give us a portion of one of the maize-bloated ducks, an especial treat, so that as we travel the duck gently digesting shall call up tender memories of the dear Sestrol family. We have a prejudice for travelling light and, already cumbered with the earthen oil-jar, we have resisted many an over-kind offer, the country putting its generous best at the feet of the benighted town-dweller. We have declined leashes of live chicken, or charges of struggling duck which we should have to slaughter in our Parisian studio. We have also declined crates of grapes, of apples, of pears and sackfuls of walnuts. No, the peasant is not always mean. A bottle of the famous walnut elixir we also refused, having tasted it once and found it wanting. But even during our stay in Janac we had been forced to withhold the addresses of our friends and relatives to all of whom Sestrol wished to post parcels of fruit.

There is a depressed bustle about the Hôtel Sestrol. All three members of the family appear and reappear in turn like the little man and woman in the weather machine; gazing at us with startled eyes as though they had seen us for the first time, or as though they feared that *this time* we would have magically disappeared. Each takes in turn to bring us a dish, Madame Sestrol serves the *soupe*, Raymond the *farci*, Monsieur Sestrol the ceremonious duck, Raymond once more with the salad, Monsieur Sestrol with the country cream cheese, Madame with the coffee. We drink a last toast in " China," which goes down into the system as warm as the sentiments of the Sestrols themselves. They are not mourning over ten francs a day, they have offered to keep us another fortnight for nothing, they have offered to put us up next year rent free if we will drop in on our way to some new untrodden land.

Is it sad to break off such friendships? Conventionally, yes: people have such short memories, they feel that to break thus means forgetfulness. But I am not so sure. We have had the best of the Sestrols, they the best of us. We have linked memories in the warm contact of a meridional summer, and in the respectful exchange of mutual liking. But how would we prosecute a closer relationship? On the whole we must be glad that the severance comes apropos, when none of life's bitter or ironic accident has had a chance to intrude between us. Now our memories of them will sit enshrined, immutable like a smiling Buddha, in a warm orange glow upon the grey blue of the already forgotten.

Cou-Cou, the baker's lad, comes to bid us good-bye. We have taken a photo of him during the fête in a group of six young people. Eagerly he asks us to send him a copy. We say that we fear it will not be a very good likeness, the sun was too strong in his eyes. He shifts on to one foot, then on to the other, blushes and says that he doesn't mind how *he* comes out, if only the young woman at his left hand—— Cou-Cou has an ordeal before him. Next spring he is booked for his military service. He is proud of this, conventionally proud, herd-instinctively proud; but a recruit without some private means has a hard time in the service. His task is of the roughest, his supplementary pay, sole resource for extra delicacies and treats, but a wretched halfpenny a day. The prospect of eighteen months under such conditions is not exciting.

The blacksmith comes up, he, too, wants a photo of himself, at the head of the procession; Monsieur Diadème also demands a picture of his donkey with the *galette* and the small grandson rampant. The old *épicier*-cobbler and his wife hobble across the *place*, they want no more than a parting shake of the hand.

The little cart with the black horse is loaded up, on go the gladstone bag, the roll of canvas and easels, the rücksack, the guitar case and the laud case, on goes a generous parcel of food for the travelling and a bottle of Sestrol's best wine. The cart, led by Monsieur Sestrol, draws away downhill, down the sinuous road which flanks the Janac promontory. We loiter a little at the hotel; take our leave of good Madame Sestrol, who weeps, murmuring in her clumsy French:

" Ça me fait peine de vous voir partir. J'étais si contente de vous, j'étais si contente de vous."

We comfort her, and at last take our leave; more hardened to such partings, and more philosophical, we nevertheless go feeling a regret that we are too English to weep in our turn.

Lemoule and his family are awaiting us round the corner; he is now in correspondence with the American re-education bureau, we promise to look up music schools for him in Paris; the baker gives us a parting grasp; Mademoiselle Cécile beams a good-bye; Monsieur " Chestnuts " waves a hand. " Come back to Janac next year," they all say, and we dare not explain that for us life depends on *not* coming back to Janac; that our Juggernaut path is strewn with the crushed corpses of such friendships. We are, alas—realists.

Reflecting over this our portrait we realize that the reader may accuse us of a certain distorting emphasis. He may say that in painting the face of Oliver Cromwell, so to speak, we have paid too much attention to the warts and too little to the countenance. Perhaps that is so, although we believe that the very texture of many of these so-called warts will imply to the intelligent the countenance behind. We may have borrowed Sestrol's method, the primitive method, we may have elaborated the detail rather too much. At least we have dressed up the puppet, please lend it the necessary life and a sufficiency of common conditions to vitalize it.

The train draws away from the station, and in the night Janac promontory, Janac village, Janac fortress are no more than as shadows cast up on to an indigo curtain. Then we plunge into a tunnel and Janac has vanished from the sight, possibly for ever. We mean to go back to Janac one day, on a flying visit, we resolve sincerely ; but may not that resolve be yet another paving-stone tumbling down to the great and ultimate causeway ?

For Product Safety Concerns and Information please contact our EU
representative GPSR@taylorandfrancis.com
Taylor & Francis Verlag GmbH, Kaufingerstraße 24, 80331 München, Germany

www.ingramcontent.com/pod-product-compliance
Lightning Source LLC
Chambersburg PA
CBHW062125300426
44115CB00012BA/1815